A PHARMGIRL ADVENTURE STORY

The ROOSTER in the DRIVE THRU

Tales of Life in the Midwest

PEGGY BADGETT

Copyrighted April 2015 by Peggy Badgett

Second Edition October 2024

All rights reserved. No part of this book may be reproduced in any form, or by any electronic, mechanical, or other means without permission in writing from the author.

Published by pharmgirlstudios

ISBN 978099159642-3

To my editor, Becky Jantz, and my cover/interior designer, Victoria Wolf for their wonderful insights and recommendations

To my father who taught me to follow my dreams

To all the friends, neighbors, and family who supported me during the lengthy process of this book's conception and birth

Most of all, to my amazing children Alex, Amie and Hannah. Without your inspiration and first editions of "Chicken Strips" these pages would be empty.

Hannah, Peggy, Amie, and Alex

Disclaimer:

This book is a collection of stories about life in the rural Midwest. Written purely from the author's perspective, some of the names and situations have been changed. The author is not responsible for any adverse consequences resulting from recipes or building maintenance methods described on these pages.

Chapter 1

"YOU'RE CRAZY TO GIVE ALL OF THIS UP!" my friend said as she scanned aisles of the huge department store inside the bustling three-story mall. Her child sat quietly in his stroller, content to gaze at colorful storefront exhibits and sip on juice. My two daughters Amie and Hannah strained against their stroller belts – and Alex, my son, had disappeared. Just when I thought my heart would pound out of my chest, Sandy spotted Alex's blond head in the toy section.

Holiday shopping, a challenge with finances already stretched thin by three children under the age of five, was not my favorite pastime. I'd already returned a scarf and two coffee mugs to their displays after seeing the prices. And I didn't like crowds. Especially when dazzling merchandise racks lured my free-spirited darlings away. Sandy and I threaded our strollers through knots of women in designer shoes and cashmere sweaters, keeping my son in sight. I felt conspicuous in my spit-up stained sweatshirt and no-name sneakers.

I quietly said "no" to Alex's hopeful expression while gently prying the yellow plastic bulldozer from his arms. After placing it back in an open spot between toy excavators, I turned to find both girls had escaped the stroller. They were chasing each other under racks of coats. Alex joined the game. I was playing a zone defense to keep them all in sight –but losing. Time to end our expedition. Check-out lines were too long anyway. It looked like I'd be hand-crafting gifts for everyone again. Unless I won the lottery. Which I never played.

Promising to call Sandy later, I hustled my brood toward the exit and loaded everyone into the van. Then I navigated the maze of tangled roads to our home. After putting the kids down for naps, I sat on our saggy couch with an old photo album and cup of tea. Jake and Ellie, our rescue dogs, hopped up beside me. A broken couch spring poked my tailbone, so I wiggled closer to Jake. Ellie slid into the uncomfortable spot and looked at me with soulful eyes. I patted her head and turned brittle pages framing Polaroid pictures. Fond memories of playing baseball with neighborhood friends, climbing mighty oak trees with my brothers, and wandering country lanes in search of plump mulberries flooded my head. There was even a photo of me beneath my favorite weeping willow. Its emerald cascade of leaves and branches had provided a quiet refuge while I read books or sketched horses in a notebook. I sighed. My children were never going experience that kind of freedom in the crowded suburbs.

The little ranch house I grew up in had one black and white television. There was no remote, and only three channels to choose from. Often, one of us children had to stand next to it as a human antenna, so the picture wasn't a grainy jumble of shapes. Voices over the pink princess telephone with ten feet of tangled cord were carried by actual wires and poles. My brothers and I were allowed an hour of watching or talking a day. And we didn't care; the country neighborhood was ours to roam. On summer mornings, we finished our chores, dashed out the door, and returned only when our mother rang the dinner bell.

During the school year, homework was our responsibility. Every afternoon we kids labored over worksheets copied from chalkboards at the dining room table while my mom cooked dinner. Good grades were expected-- and delivered. My favorite grade school memory was of a fourth-grade teacher who read classic novels aloud in class. It was usually after lunch on Wednesdays. Half the class nodded off at their desks, but I listened raptly to every word. Sometimes I even borrowed the paperback from him because I couldn't wait a week to hear what happened next. That love of literature was reinforced at home; my mother was an avid bookworm. We visited the local library often. Books transported me to places far beyond barbed wire fences and cornfields, sparking my imagination and dreams.

Mathematical equations and the biology of living creatures fascinated me in junior high. I was a nerd in glasses, braces, and braids. During that time, my father bought a natural foods store. We were all expected to help. After school, I ran the cash register and stocked shelves. Over time, my father taught me how to sell products and manage the store, grooming me to take over the business when he retired. I became known as the "health food store girl." The growing nutrition industry and interest in supplements assured a good life in that small town. But the seductive lure of adventure encouraged me to leave vitamin bottles and cow pastures behind. An exciting world lay just outside our small city limits. I wanted to experience it.

Part-time jobs, loans, and scholarships paid for my college education. After six years of immersion in biology, chemistry, calculus, and pharmacology, I proudly walked across the stage to receive my pharmacy diploma. Ours was the first class where women equaled the number of male graduates, and pharmacists were in demand. Offers of retail positions in Texas and California enticed me, but my interest was piqued by two research opportunities. I chose the one in the glamorous suburbs of Chicago.

A company-sponsored moving truck deposited eight boxes of clothes, several puppy posters, a small dresser, and a bed in my first apartment.

The men chuckled as they worked; it was probably one of the easiest jobs they had ever done. After unpacking, I explored the luxurious living complex's heated swimming pool, tennis courts, and walking paths around landscaped ponds. It was unlike anything I'd ever lived in. There were no cows or soybeans in sight.

I quickly settled into my career, managing projects and meetings. New friends introduced me to ethnic restaurants, dance clubs, theaters, and fascinating museums on the weekends. While my hometown friends married their high school sweethearts, had babies, and bought minivans, I traveled to exotic places and purchased a sleek sports car. I was a free spirit and determined to remain that way.

Years passed. Fate chose a different plot over my plan and sent me stumbling into the arms of a handsome man on a dance floor one night. I never was graceful in high heels. A little voice in my head whispered he was the one, and a whirlwind courtship followed. My free-spirit-career-self caught a jet to the tropics as we repeated our vows in a big white church filled with family and friends.

After a honeymoon cruise, we settled into comfortable cohabitation. While climbing our respective company ladders, we cheered Chicago sports teams, played golf on beautiful suburban courses, and joined a sand volleyball league. Then the little voice in my head started to whisper again. I couldn't quite hear what she was saying, until one morning when I went out for a jog and almost ran over a man picking up his golden retriever's poop. Suddenly her message was clear. It was time to become a parent. To a dog. I had grown up with black Labradors, Irish Setters, and every kind of mutt in between; I missed their companionship. My old apartment hadn't allowed pets, but there were no such rules at our condo. It seemed like everyone in our neighborhood walked behind wagging tails except us. So, we adopted a collie mix who had been rescued near a large dumpster by a friend of a friend. The young mutt was wild and his placement with a temporary home was tenuous. After gazing into those big brown eyes, I volunteered to be his forever mom. His foster parent quickly loaded him into my car with a bag of kibble before I changed my mind.

We named him Jake. In the first seven days, Jake gnawed through four pairs of designer heels, two video game controllers, and six trashy romance novels. So, we crated him when we were gone and took him for lots of walks to make up for his imprisonment. But my feeble commands of "heel" went unheeded as he sprinted gleefully from tree to tree, towing me in his wake. One night he slipped free from his collar and dashed into the woods. After yelling his name for thirty minutes, I sadly walked home with an empty leash. Jake returned to the condo an hour later, full of burrs and reeking of skunk. After his tomato juice bath, our shower walls were splattered with bright red streaks. The bathroom looked like a murder scene. Industrial cleaners didn't even fade the stains. It took three coats of paint to cover them.

One of my coworkers recommended a dog trainer who was legendary in his ability to perform miracles. I enrolled us in the beginning obedience session with high hopes. But by the end of our second class, the instructor threw his hands up in dismay and proclaimed us both discipline disasters. So, when we bought our first house, we made sure it had a nice yard for our dog to run in. Run Jake did, right out our back yard, through the neighbors' gates, and into the great wide open. We spent hours hunting him, uttering choice words while calling his name. He always found his way back to the front porch before we did.

Realizing it was going to be tough to teach him to stay in a small area after he had roamed freely, we thought a companion might keep him closer to home. A fence would have been cheaper and less work. Ellie came to us from another friend of a friend, who had adopted a puppy after their children promised to take care of her. The kids lost interest in three days. We took her in. Jake and Ellie got along famously. But we discovered that the diabolical naughtiness did not double with two canine minds; it quadrupled. I learned a lot of new bad words. Jake and Ellie ran away often, and when they finally returned home after treeing every squirrel in the neighborhood, there were double the number of burrs to pluck from their fur. But despite all the exasperation our dogs caused, I loved them.

One morning, after skidding through trash the dogs had dug from the tamper-proof bin again, my cheek connected with the countertop edge. In a bad way. As I held a bag of frozen peas to the blossoming bruise, my reflection in the bathroom mirror startled me. The bruise was scary, but even more horrifying was the growing network of crow's feet and laugh lines on my face. The whispering influencer in my head that had goaded me into matrimony and canine parenthood spoke clearly at that moment. Trusting she was not leading me down the wrong path this time, I followed her directions and tossed my birth control pills in the trash. My manager had just outlined his plan to fast track me into management. I crossed my fingers and hoped my body would determine the best future for me.

Our first child was greeted with enthusiasm and cautious curiosity. We dragged Alex everywhere as we vainly tried to maintain our B.C. (Before Children) lifestyle. It worked until he became mobile. Alex always wore a slightly concerned expression, as if he knew I had no clue how to be a mother. I switched from full-time research work to half-time project leadership. Twenty months after Alex's birth, the walls of our home closed in even more after our second child, Amie, arrived kicking and squalling.

Nine months later, the pregnancy test screamed positive as I burped Amie over my shoulder. I sat heavily on the bed next to Ellie in amazement. How had I, the adventurous career girl from the country who had denounced marriage and children, landed in suburbia expecting my third infant? My free-spirit-career-self shrieked in horror and commandeered a sailboat headed to ports unknown. Seven months later, on a beautiful September morning, Hannah burst into our world.

When my final maternity leave ended, day care costs for three kids under the age of five outweighed my part-time salary. I quit my research position and donated my corporate suits to a homeless shelter. Wading through days of keeping tiny clothes, sippy cups, and baby bottoms clean became my new career. But parenthood was a gigantic puzzle for me. Not one of our delightful offspring had arrived with scientific standard operating procedures or protocols. Muddling through the complexities of Alex's potty training, Amie's temper tantrums in aisle three of the grocery store, and Hannah's refusal to sleep reinforced my feelings of inadequacy as a mother.

Excursions with three young children were limited due to complicated traveling logistics. The diaper bag loaded with emergency supplies alone weighed ten pounds. There were many days I did not see an adult soul. I missed my coworkers. Any aspirations of being a gracefully calm mother went out the window. Basic survival was my only goal as the whirlpool of babyhood sucked me under.

In desperation, I signed up for a mom and tot class through the local park district. After our first meeting, those wonderful women became a lifeline to sanity. I wasn't alone in my fears and worries. We gathered weekly after the class ended for fellowship and mutual support. Our friendships helped unravel the mystery of motherhood and forge a path through all the confusing parenting advice.

The small suburb we lived had grown as quickly as our family. Subdivisions of cookie cutter houses swallowed the once rich farmland. We resided in an ocean of shingled roofs, broken only by an occasional ancient white oak that miraculously survived the bulldozers. Brightly colored playgrounds swarmed with intimidating older kids commanding the best slides and swings. The simple task of buying groceries took hours to load and unload children, pile food around them in a squeaky metal cart, and wait in line behind ten other families.

Urban life lost its charm after I became a mother. We didn't go to sporting events anymore, and my golf clubs sat forgotten in the garage. If we braved a table at the local pizzeria, maintaining peace between three little kids necessitated most of my attention. By the time I picked up a fork, my slice was cold and congealed. Hiking through forest preserves with the dogs had been an easy escape when I needed a dose of nature B.C. But trying to juggle a stroller with a baby, toddler, an inquisitive five-year old, and two disobedient dogs was almost impossible. I felt edgy, despite the companionship of my motherhood friends, old co-workers, and wonderful neighbors.

The voice that had led me to six years of incubating and lactating began to whisper again every time we visited my hometown (my free-spirit-career-self was silent and still sailing around the world.) As miles rolled beneath our minivan's wheels, the suburban crush of humanity was replaced by wide open spaces. Stores and shops were pleasantly uncrowded. Restaurants and theaters were comfortable and inexpensive; no one minded if our kids made noise because other kids were running wild too. Parks offered empty swings, open climbing structures, and an old, red fire engine to play on. Alex, Amie, and Hannah had room to stretch their little legs. After each trip, my disenchantment with suburbia grew a little bit stronger.

My patience snapped one day as we waited our turn at a busy video rental store. Alex and Amie whined and clung to my legs. Hannah screamed on my hip; she had left her beloved blanket in the van. Tears rolled down my cheeks as others in line backed away without losing their places. I cut in front of the person at the counter, placed two movies in the hands of the bewildered check-out boy, and fled with my children. After loading everyone back into their car seats, I pointed the van toward home. It was only a mile away, but the town's five new stoplights slowed traffic to a crawl. Trapped in a long line of bumpers, we stopped and started, stopped and started, stopped and started. In the rear-view mirror, three small, troubled faces stared back at me.

By the time we pulled into our driveway, my decision was made. I was done being just another urban mom vying for parking spots at strip malls. I wanted my children to grow up with dirt under their fingernails and the freedom to roam. That whispering voice had won again. Even my free-spirit-career-self approved from her dock in Bermuda: moving to the country was as close to grand adventure a mom like me was going to get. My friends could not dissuade me. Undeterred by the many unknowns and what-ifs, we began our quest for a home in rural America.

Chapter 2

ALEX AND AMIE SQUEALED WITH LAUGHTER as they ran around the kitchen table showering the floor with shredded editorials. We perused the real estate guide from the Sunday newspaper insert, making notes in the margins. There was a haven and accompanying business to support our family somewhere in the country: we just had to find it. I almost offered Hannah my coffee as she tossed cereal to Jake and Ellie from her highchair. I caught myself just in time; the last thing we needed was caffeinated children. Suddenly, wedged between farm and ranch properties listed for sale, I spotted an advertisement for a rural pharmacy. It sounded perfect; peaceful country living while providing a vital smalltown health care service. I immediately grabbed the telephone and set up an appointment.

Five days later, we dragged the children on a six-hour road trip to southwestern Iowa. Picturesque countryside sprinkled with red and white barns, clapboard houses, and dense woodlands surrounded the small town. When the little bell over the drug store door announced our arrival, two middle-aged women clucked over our offspring and whisked Hannah from my arms. Alex and Amie raced to the toy aisle.

We walked back to the pharmacy and introduced ourselves. The pharmacist abandoned his typewriter and scooped ice cream into three dishes at the soda fountain. Alex, Amie, and Hannah perched on red spinning stools and spooned into their sundaes; the women hovered with napkins ready. While our brood was happily occupied, the pharmacist/owner toured us around the building and outlined the terms of sale on a prescription pad.

His price was reasonable and well within our reach. Homes in the area were affordable and the small town's schools were excellent. As the kids licked their spoons clean, the women recommended a visit to a brand-new community playground assembled by the town's parent-teacher organization. We thanked them for watching over our little flock, shook hands with the pharmacist, and promised to call with our decision. Then we walked to the park. I pushed Hannah in a baby swing while Alex and Amie raced through brightly colored slides, tiny forts, and climbing spots. The steady chugging of a tractor announced a farmer spreading manure in a field nearby. Its earthy scent drifted toward us on the soft breeze.

It was easy to envision a pleasant life there. We could cheer local sports teams on and volunteer at the schools. Small town pharmacists were usually on the front line of health care, advising patients to see a doctor when necessary or recommending first aid supplies when it wasn't. I would have the chance to become an integral part of the community. However, mile after mile of endless corn fields on the way back to the suburbs proved the location too remote. Our purpose was to move away from the city and crowds, not drop off the edge of the world. It was just too far from family.

We found another intriguing business/home option in the newspaper the next weekend. It was a dog boarding kennel in southern Wisconsin, just a few hours over the Illinois border. The shorter drive resulted in a lot less protests from the back seat gallery. But the rough condition of the facility and attached home was apparent even to our novice eyes. Plus, we could barely manage our small dog herd of two, let alone thirty more. Over a chorus of barking and howling, we thanked the owners for their time and hustled the kids to the van.

There were plenty of rural properties without attached businesses for sale in Northwest Illinois. We decided to focus there because retail pharmacies always had openings. So, in an ironic twist of fate, we left the suburbs once a month to view real estate in the area I had sworn never to return to. But after each tour of barren fields, raccoon-infested homes, and dilapidated buildings, we realized translation was necessary for the creative writing allowed in real estate descriptions. "Charming old home" meant rotted beams and sagging floors, "beautiful views" included dead trees visible from grimy windows, and "sturdy outbuildings" encompassed structures tilting earthward. We needed professional help. Especially after we found ourselves lost on a dirt road surrounded by bleating sheep one Saturday morning.

We contacted a realtor to arrange monthly showings for us. She would ensure the properties we viewed were within our price range and have indoor plumbing and viable outbuildings. We drove west with the kids, dogs, and high hopes again. The first parcel our realtor showed us boasted a setting of mature red oaks surrounding a "stately" residence. The home turned out to be a small cabin with an outdoor kitchen, the trees were on an adjacent property, and the only outbuilding was a rusted metal shed filled with broken machinery. We crossed that one off the list. The next candidate was an old farmhouse undergoing a complete renovation. We loved the house, but scraggly weeds were the only vegetation poking through five acres of red clay and rock surrounding it. Amie and Hannah both screamed as I buckled them back into their car seats. After Jake stole Alex's granola bar, I waved the white flag, surrendered to their demands of ice cream and a park, and promised our realtor we would return the next month.

Thirty days later, we began our tour at a farm nestled in a small valley. Our excitement grew as we toured the charming old house. Its rooms and spacious kitchen were exactly what I had hoped for. Then my spirits plummeted when we ventured down the basement stairs. An ancient spring bubbled through a trench and flowed out into the back yard. The farm's water source. Our realtor told us exposed wells were not uncommon, but I couldn't shake visions of drowned children and dogs from my head. After that, we drove by several candidates on tiny plots of land without even stopping. The final property she showed us that weekend had beautiful, wooded hillsides and a meandering creek. But the home was a weathered double wide trailer with peeling wallpaper and exposed wiring.

Months of twisting ankles in rough pastures and tiptoeing through dingy houses left us discouraged. Even with expert assistance, our dream home still seemed unattainable. Then one weekend we followed our realtor down a tree-lined lane to a large dairy farm. The owner was selling it in separate parcels. One was ten acres with the barn and house. The remaining one hundred acres was offered as crop land. The two-story clapboard house had a large bathroom, and the bedrooms were light and airy. The master showcased a window seat overlooking rolling hills of corn and beans. The only defect was a lack of dishwasher, but I eyed my three children thoughtfully. They could be trained, unlike Jake and Ellie. The wooden barn was clean and well-maintained, and a wide creek flowed through the partially wooded ten-acre pasture. It was perfect.

We signed a contract to purchase the ten acres, barn, and home. Elated, I immediately told our friends and family the exciting news. Then a few days later we received a devastating telephone call. One of our realtor's clients had submitted an offer to purchase both parcels together, the entire farm. Outbidding them wasn't an option. My dream had been hijacked by our own agent.

We found a new broker. While Amie, Alex, and Hannah thundered up and down her office hallway, she wrote down our requirements. Then she set up appointments to visit at least four places meeting most of our criteria during each hunting trip. Trying to keep up with her on the winding dusty roads kept our children entertained. Alex, Amie, and Hannah adored their "wild realtor lady." Enthusiastic once more, we continued our quest as farm-hunting weekend warriors.

We explored properties near every small town within one hundred miles, but nothing piqued our interested enough to make an offer. The further south we explored, the flatter the land became. Telephone and electric poles provided the only relief between alfalfa fields. We liked the landscape better up north. One weekend, our realtor led us to a place we had visited six months before. Then, the buildings had held a jumble of rusty implements, and the house had been filled with plaster dust from major restorations. As we pulled into the lane, it was love at second sight. All the work inside the Victorian home had been completed. An extensive front porch invited lounging on summer days. Sunlight streamed through unusually large windows in every room. Outbuildings were ready for livestock. A small creek wound its way through the thistle-filled twenty-acre pasture. The little voice of discontentment wholeheartedly approved. Even my free-spirit-career-self docked in Aruba grudgingly gave a thumbs up. After nine months of tromping through the Midwest, we had found our sanctuary.

My brother Randy, a self-taught carpenter who ran the health food store I'd grown up in, inspected the main structures for us. He did not find any major defects. And the water source was an underground well covered by a heavy cement lid. The actual construction date of the house was unknown, but the barn evidenced hand-hewn timbers and wooden pegs circa 1920's. This time our transaction to buy the little farm proceeded smoothly, fueled by bankers and title officers who knew my family as well as friends I had gone to grade school with.

Closing on our new property took all of twenty minutes. That included herding the kids back into the room several times when they made a break for it. After we signed the final document and disarmed Alex, Amie, and Hannah of pilfered pens, we celebrated at an old-fashioned ice cream parlor. My lemon sorbet puddled around the dish while I wiped the chins and fingers of our five-year-old son, three-year-old daughter, and eighteen-month toddler. I didn't mind. Then we drove to our new farm and unlocked the door for the first time. On the crumbling sidewalk leading up to the farmhouse back door, Alex, Amie, and Hannah discovered a litter of kittens who were batting at line of marching ants. Jake and Ellie dozed in shady dirt beds beneath one of the ancient silver maples in our yard. A neighbor drove past on his red tractor and waved. Barn swallows swooped over the shaggy grass and rode the breeze back up, drawing my attention to wispy clouds floating in the deep blue sky. A cow lowed in the distance. I sighed with happiness.

Eventually the kittens decided they had been handled enough, were hungry, and mewed pitifully at their mother. I'd been petting her on the front porch step. She gave me a look of conspiratorial exasperation, trotted to her babies, and lay down so they could each reach a nipple. Alex, Amie, and Hannah ran to me, begging for snacks as well. Thankful their nursing stages were over, I reminded them they had just had ice cream and sent them off to pick dandelions.

Clyde, the gentlemanly golden Labrador who had been included with our rural purchase, was the undisputed ruler of our little kingdom. He took his job seriously and patrolled the boundaries of the farm for unwanted intruders like raccoons and ground hogs. Clyde took Alex, Amie, and Hannah on as his protected charges and watched over them almost better than I did.

Keeping one eye on the kids and dogs, we began to assess our new property. I scribbled notes on a yellow legal pad. Looking through my "mom" eyes instead of the "how-romantic-we-are-moving-to-the-country" eyes made some issues startlingly apparent. The list of "Potential Deadly Hazards" included several urgent child-proofing issues. That was followed by a list of "Projects Requiring Professional Help" for things like rewiring electrical outlets and updating the plumbing. There were projects I thought I could manage on my own, like painting and patching. Those were on my "Do It Myself" or DIM list (yeah, pretty sure there was a message there). Finally, I compiled a list of "Expensive Items to be Funded After We Win the Lottery": replacement fencing and a new roof for the barn. Overwhelmed, I joined Alex, Amie, and Hannah to look for a four-leafed clover. We were going to need some luck.

I herded the kids and dogs back into the van, and patted Clyde goodbye. The neighbor who owned the cows grazing our pasture had offered to feed and care for him until we were permanently moved. Beautiful shades of violet and pink colored the horizon behind us as we drove back to the suburbs. Soon I would admire those sunsets from our front porch instead of the rear-view mirror. Stuffing the lists out of sight, I turned the radio to a children's music station. The kids nodded off ten miles into the drive, exhausted by the country fresh air and sunshine.

It had been a long, exciting weekend. After depositing everyone into bed, I sat down with a cold bottle of chardonnay and the yellow legal pad. The list of "Potential Deadly Hazards" needed to be addressed first. Our grand Victorian house presented a myriad of safety issues. Stairs leading to the bedrooms were horribly steep and covered in slippery, frayed carpeting. Electrical outlets were within easy reach of curious fingers holding keys. The front porch with its spectacular view had no rails to stop a four-foot fall to the cement-like ground below. The barn and outbuildings were filled with rusty nails, rotted lumber, and siding pieces angled precariously against the walls. Glass shards from splintered windowpanes littered the dirt and rocks around every foundation. There was emergency room potential everywhere.

It took a month of weekend clean-ups to finish the critical projects we hoped would keep us away from the hospital. I picked up countless buckets of sharp, tetanus-inducing items while sprinting to check on the children every five minutes. A sturdy plastic gate kept them off the steep stairs, and boards hammered between posts along the front porch blocked swan dives over the edge. Frequent breaks to go for walks on the nearby country fire lane or play kickball in the front yard balanced the cleaning drudgery. By Sunday afternoon, our van was stuffed with bulging black contractor bags full of trash. We barely had room for the cooler, kids, Jake, and Ellie. Before we drove away, I always gave Clyde a hug and instructed him to be good for our dog-sitting neighbor. Back in suburbia, we carried sleeping kids to their beds, sent Jake and Ellie into the backyard to do their business, unloaded the van, and collapsed onto the couch.

Once the farm was relatively free from the worst hazards, we picked a moving date in August. My focus shifted to packing. One afternoon, as I begged Hannah to open her mouth for a spoonful of mashed peas, Alex and Amie slipped Jake and Ellie quartered hot dog pieces. They thought I didn't know. I grinned. The little suburban house had become tight quarters for our tribe but held many precious memories. Scrapbooks from those years were the first items to be gently placed in bins.

It was a monumental task getting our family ready to move. That was on top of feeding, cleaning, potty training, diaper changing, and cooking. Nap time was never long enough to make much progress. I needed to get the kids involved, and bribery was my best lure. Dangling the promise of candy once we packed two containers, I identified kitchen items that were ready for boxing. Alex and Amie wrapped them in newspaper, then Hannah put the objects inside boxes. Luckily most of our housewares were not valuable. The kids did well for a while. Then Alex told Amie she was doing it wrong. She wadded the society page into a ball and threw it at him. He retaliated with a shot of balled-up sports stats to her head.

Hannah hid behind her blanket as it escalated to all-out war. I tripped over a hidden plastic bowl and dropped my favorite earthenware platter. After counting to ten five times, I turned on the television, handed out treats, and hired a neighborhood teenager to watch the kids while I packed alone.

Once the cabinets were empty, Alex and Amie used them to play peek-a-boo with Hannah. She squealed with delight every time they popped out. Then they dug out their favorite pots, pans, and wooden spoons from my just-packed containers. At least they weren't bored. I gave up and left the kitchen symphony to clean out the downstairs bedroom. When I threw several old but treasured dance club outfits into a bag destined for a homeless shelter, my free-spirit-career-self screamed in protest. I defiantly added the last pair of my designer shoes. Then I heard giggling inside one of the boxes. Hannah had crawled inside again. I sighed, took everyone for a walk around the block, and wondered what I could fix for dinner. Our wonderful neighbor saved us from starvation with her famous "Nana's chicken casserole."

Some dear friends threw an old-fashioned, going-away barbecue for us, even importing straw bales for seating from their parents' farm in central Illinois. All my old co-workers attended. A lump lodged in my throat as we reminisced about past adventures. Alex, Amie, and Hannah plucked pieces of straw out of the bales and tossed them in the air, making us all itch and sneeze. At the end of the evening, I corralled the children and tearfully said goodbye to everyone.

The most difficult people to part with were my playgroup mom mentors. Our last hours together felt like precious grains of sand slipping through my fingers. At our final gathering, there were no dry eyes, lots of tight hugs, and earnest vows to keep in touch. Those women had rescued me from the brink of motherhood disaster. Would I survive parenting at the edge of civilization without them?

As the circled calendar date crept closer, I tossed and turned at night. Canceling utilities, starting utilities, and changing addresses along with countless other things needing to be done spun together like a cyclone in my mind. When we weren't packing, I snapped photographs of Alex, Amie, and Hannah playing at our favorite playgrounds. Then I pushed them in the stroller to the Tastee Freeze where they giggled and dripped ice cream everywhere. I knew I would miss the convenience of those places once we moved to the middle of nowhere; suburbia did have its good points. Our neighbors

Moving day dawned sunny and warm. We picked up our truck as soon as the rental place opened. Several friends arrived to help, along with our babysitter who kept kids and dogs clear of the adult traffic. At first, it appeared as if our belongings would only occupy a tiny portion of the cavernous space. Boxes, furniture, and toys artfully balanced in neat rows. But the truck quickly reached capacity, and we shut the back door before the final row could tumble out. Our neighbor delivered warm chocolate chip cookies and lemonade that we gratefully devoured. After our break, we carefully wedged lamps, plants, and breakable items into the van. Then we hugged our helpers good-bye while Jake and Ellie hopped into the van and curled up on bedding in between the kids' car seats. Several tears rolled down my face as I put the van into drive. Pieces of our lives were the only things visible in the rear-view mirror as we headed west.

When the van and truck rumbled up the gravel lane of our new home, my high school friend Julie and husband Ron were waiting. Clyde also greeted us, wagging his tail nonstop. Their daughters took our three kids for a walk while we set up the ramp bridging the front porch to the truck tailgate. Jake and Ellie extricated themselves from the van and raced inside the house instead of running off to find something disgusting to roll in. Grown-ups formed an assembly line between the truck and house, moving stacks from outside in. Halfway through unloading, the kids returned. I sent them off to pick violets and clover. Clyde followed them. In two hours, the moving vehicles were hollow vessels, and our farmhouse was filled with boxes. Everyone was starving.

I opened a box labeled silverware and dishes in the kitchen, only to discover winter boots instead. One of the hazards of packing with small children. Then a miracle appeared. One of our new neighbors delivered large containers of food along with paper plates and plastic silverware. I thanked her profusely as she headed back home to milk their cows, unearthed the cooler filled with drinks, and called everyone to dinner. After mounding plates with ham, fruit, and potato salad, we sat on the front yard in mismatched lawn chairs and admired the view. There were no scraps left for the tom cats who circled us and meowed pitifully.

After dinner, Julie and Ron left with their exhausted girls. Jake and Ellie sprawled amid the boxes in the dining room. Clyde took up his post on the front porch. Alex, Amie, Hannah, and I retrieved pajamas from our suitcases and set up camp in the living room on our pull-out sofa sleeper. I nestled into the warmth of three small bodies around me. Crickets chirped outside the big picture window, and somewhere in the distance an owl hooted softly. Just as my eyelids flickered shut, coyotes yipped excitedly. It sounded like they were in our front yard. Clyde woofed a few times in answer. I bolted upright, counted noses to make sure everyone was accounted for, and smiled. Maybe rural areas weren't as quiet as I had imagined, but it was better than sirens and honking horns. I quickly fell asleep.

Nana's Chicken Casserole

2 c. broasted chicken
1 c. grated carrot
1 c. cream of celery soup
1 c. mayonaise
½ c. butter

½ c. chopped onion
1 c. chopped celery
1 c. cooked brown rice
crushed butter crackers
tarragon or thyme

Preheat oven at 350°. Grease 13x9 pan. Saute veggies in butter (2T.) until soft. Add soup, shredded chicken, rice and spices + mayonaise. Spread in pan. Top with crushed crackers & drizzle w/ melted butter. Bake 30-40 min. until golden.

Chapter 3

OUR FIRST COUNTRY WEEK PASSED in a flurry of trying to keep everyone safe, fed, and clean. And that was only the children. Jake and Ellie quickly discovered how to wiggle out of their collars when tied out. After their romps through the countryside, I washed whatever they had found to roll in that day with cold well water from the hose. Clyde did his best to watch over the kids, but every time I turned my head, someone was running with a sharp object that had evaded our pre-move safety clean-ups. It was only after everyone was tucked in for the night that I collapsed on the couch and hoped tomorrow would be a better day.

Thinking a little order in our new household might alleviate my feeling of being besieged, I decided to organize the kitchen. Alex, Amie, and Hannah were starting to roll their eyes at peanut butter and jelly sandwiches. Not that they wanted broccoli or Brussel sprouts. Just some noodles to break the monotony. So, the kids stacked plastic containers inside a cabinet while I concentrated on finding a home for dishes and glasses. Pots and pans found homes in lower spots. Then we arranged canned fruit, vegetables, and boxes of pasta on shelves in the pantry. The enormous accomplishment was celebrated with an apple juice toast and macaroni and cheese.

It was time to settle everyone into bedrooms. Our slumber parties had been fun for two nights. Then, reality set in. Amie kicked my shins when she rolled over, Hannah poked my ribs with her stuffed seal, and Alex mumbled in his sleep. We marched upstairs to survey the options. Alex claimed the middle bedroom, Amie and Hannah chose the long narrow one, and I was left with one overlooking the barn and pasture. After I shuffled and tugged respective beds to their new homes, I spent an entire morning assembling Alex's bunk bed with my new power screwdriver only to discover upon completion I'd assembled it backwards. He was content with a mattress on the floor. Hannah's crib popped together, and Amie had an old twin bed with one-way slats I couldn't put together wrong.

Three nights later, Hannah woke up crying. Her little body radiated heat. Carrying her downstairs, I shuffled slowly through the rooms to avoid tripping over plastic blocks. The screen door slapped shut behind us as I settled into a rickety aluminum lawn chair and held her. Thunder rumbled and lightning flickered in the distance. Tears of exhaustion trickled down my cheeks. We weren't unpacked, and I had no idea how to approach the vast amount of work facing me while parenting three young children and two wayward mutts. There were so many rural skills I needed to master. It appeared hopeless. Clyde nosed my face as if he understood and lay down next to our chair with a sigh.

When the sun rose over the hill, I winced and gently stretched my aching back. Hannah's fever raged. After pouring cereal into bowls for Alex and Amie, I rocked Hannah on my hip and made a desperate phone call to Julie. Her pediatrician's nurse squeezed us into the schedule. When we arrived at the office, Amie stumbled, fell to the floor, and began crying at the sight of her rug burn. Hannah joined. We were quickly ushered into an examination room. The girls sobbed even harder when the doctor opened the door. He peeked into Hannah's ears and diagnosed a double ear infection. As he finished his evaluation of her lungs (quite healthy based on her screams), he handed me antibiotic samples and instructions. While he completed his chart notes, he asked if we were new in town. I babbled about how we had made this romantic move from the suburbs to the country and that it was a lot more work than I had thought and started crying myself.

The doctor clucked sympathetically, patted my shoulder, and handed me tissues. As I dried my face and mopped Amie's and Hannah's tears, he advised me to relax and enjoy my children while they were young. Smiling as he left the room, I figured he was probably thankful his kids were adults. I paid our bill at the front desk as Alex and Amie clung to my legs and Hannah sniffed under her blanket. A very pregnant woman and her husband sat in the waiting room and watched us with wide deer-in-the-headlight eyes.

Back at the dusty old van, I buckled everyone into their car seats and took a deep breath. The doctor had prescribed an adjustment of expectations. He was right. The antibiotics worked magic on Hannah's infection. She slept through the night after four doses. I changed my tactics and quit writing unattainable goals for each day. We settled into a new routine. After breakfast, the kids played with toys while I distributed items from a box or two. Naptime followed lunch. I dozed with the dogs. After snack time, we prepared for our afternoon walk. I leashed Jake and Ellie, coaxed the girls into the stroller, grabbed Alex's hand, and followed Clyde's waving tail down the gravel road. We dropped rocks into the creek at the bottom of the hill, picked Queen Anne's Lace, and counted starlings lined up on the telephone lines. After dinner, Alex and Amie stood on chairs at the kitchen sink to wash dishes. Hannah and I dried. Then it was bath time in the pink cast iron tub. Finally story time with a book for each child. After everyone was tucked into their own beds,

I scribbled a reasonable to-do list for the next day before nodding off myself. There were still a lot of mornings I awoke to three small bodies snuggled next to me. But I savored those moments instead of racing to clean up the garbage Jake and Ellie had distributed again.

Clyde moved inside with us at the end of our second week. I couldn't stand the unfairness of shutting the door on his gentle amber eyes every evening, even though his doghouse was quite nice. The Labrador's calm demeanor was a wonderful contrast to Jake and Ellie's spirited races through the house with stolen socks and underwear. I often discovered Hannah curled up asleep on Clyde's golden shoulder in the afternoon.

If our to-do list dictated errands in town, we included a visit to Julie's house or my brother's place. The kids played with other kids, and I held a conversation about something other than fruit snacks. When we stayed home, we held tea parties on blankets in the front yard or built blanket tents with couch cushions in the living room. If I became stressed about making the farm a model home or being a perfect mom, I just looked out one of our windows. The panoramic view of the land soothed my soul - until one of the children informed me Clyde had again eaten the chocolate chip cookies cooling on the counter.

I thanked a neighbor for her pretty pink cupcakes one afternoon while body blocking Jake and Ellie's escape at the back porch door. After waving goodbye, I returned to the kitchen. My children were drawing crayon pictures at the table without fighting over robin egg blue or forest green. A fistful of violets sat on the table in a jelly jar. Tomato sauce simmered beside a pot of spaghetti noodles. I put the cupcakes in the refrigerator, out of Clyde's reach. Country life was good.

Chapter 4

THE CHARM OF OWNING OLD BARNS, sheds, and land faded when I realized the vast amount of attention they required. It was all related to an important scientific principle concerning country life that had not been discussed in any of my college physics classes. The law of rural maintenance states that the hours spent keeping buildings in good repair and whitewashed were infinitely greater than the amount of time enjoying them. Slapping paint on weathered wood surfaces was fun and easy, until fights broke out about which child had the better brush. I relied on help and instruction from my brother Randy on more complicated repairs, who was always gracious with his time and tools.

Mother Nature proved relentless in her destruction once she found a way inside one of our buildings. She sent a large tree limb through a clear panel on a shed roof right after we moved in. It was far better to invest a little effort and replace the panel immediately rather than pay for professionals to re-roof the entire building in a year. The next Sunday morning, I had tools and ladders assembled when Randy arrived.

After my third climb up the ladder to deposit supplies, the children appeared at the bottom. They were bored with the kittens. I climbed down and ushered Alex, Amie, and Hannah into the house. Content with pudding cups and a movie, the kids were safely occupied for at least a half hour. I went back outside, up the ladder, and scuttled across the slick aluminum roof to my station near to the hole. Randy hauled the new panel up, sliding it towards me as he followed. Its sharp edges made me grateful for my gloves. Even though it was cool, sweat dripped down my back. I felt nauseous every time I looked down. Once the panel was in place, we quickly nailed our respective sides down before the wind flung it to the ground.

My brother casually walked to the roof edge, tossed his tools to the ground, and climbed down the ladder. He made it look easy. I broke three fingernails crawling and sliding after him. The wooden rungs shook until I reached solid ground. Randy graciously hid his laughter as we washed up and put tools back into his truck.

Alex, Amie, and Hannah, finished with their movie, were blowing bubbles on the sidewalk. I grinned and joined them, watching shimmering transparent globes float away on the breeze. Sitting beside Hannah on the cool cement, I plucked dandelions from the grass and weaved them together in a chain. When I placed the finished circlet on top of her brown curls, Amie asked for one too. I got halfway through hers when Jake trotted into the yard with something in his mouth. I chased him, but he merely ran in circles with teeth clenched on his prize. Finally, I got close enough to grab his neck and dragged him back to his tie out. After tugging the decayed raccoon carcass from his mouth, I trudged to the shed for a shovel and sent the kids inside to wash up for lunch.

We began to alternate walking the gravel road in the afternoons with exploring our property. Twenty acres was a lot of land to take care of. Gnarled crab apple trees grew along the pasture fence lines, and red-winged blackbirds chattered warnings when we walked too close to their nests. It was like having our very own private park (if barren land featuring thousands of cow manure mines could be considered a playground). At least we had the creek. The meandering little waterway wound all the way through our land. Multiple springs hidden deep in the ground kept it fluid even under the hot August sun. On our way to its banks, frequent stops along the way were required to examine interesting weeds, listen for pheasants, or watch red-tailed hawks soar above us.

The cows that grazed in our pasture watched us warily while nibbling grass and clover but left our noisy crew alone. They probably thought we were crazy when we laughingly slid down the loose dirt into the water time after time. I held onto Hannah's hand and kept Amie within reach as we waded in the water. The creek was not deep enough to pose an actual threat, but its current moved quickly. Alex laughed at the sucking sounds the mud made before it released his boots. We gathered smooth rocks from its bed and built small dams. Water bugs magically skipped along the surface and rejected the tiny boats of leaves we made for them. Clyde always hopped in the water with us and drenched everyone when he shook his fur.

Mud and red clay were ground into our clothes during our creek excursions. But I didn't mind. It was more important to introduce Alex, Amie, and Hannah to the wonderful, mysterious world around us than worry about laundry. We weren't alone. Every time we ventured into our new town, we noticed that local farmers wore their chore boots and stained overalls out and about. It explained the faint scent of manure always present in the local bank.

One afternoon, we discovered a gigantic cottonwood tree that stood beside a sweeping curve in the stream. It reminded me of the weeping willow from my childhood. Four springs bubbled up from the ground around its roots. I named her Mother Cottonwood. Judging by the width of her trunk (I couldn't fit my arms even halfway around it), I figured her life spanned well over a century. It became my favorite shady spot to lounge, watch the kids play, and let Jake and Ellie wade in the cool water. That towering tree had witnessed many changes over time. I made a solemn vow to her that I would research ways of returning our land to a more natural state instead of the trampled, hoof-pocked field it was. We had plenty of room for a wildlife sanctuary.

My daydreaming was cut short when Clyde nudged me with his large nose. He trotted behind me as I dashed off to rescue Hannah, whose boots were stuck in the mud again. It was time to gather my crew and head back to the house for dinner, baths, and bed. I was the one most exhausted.

Chapter 5

OUR CLAN HAD INCREASED THE POPULATION of our small town by almost one percent. We became the focus of much speculation instead of just another anonymous young family waiting in line to buy diapers. Especially when I picked out groceries from the small town's store in grass-stained jeans with three mud-streaked children trailing behind me. Even though we blended in clothing-wise, we still had some suburban habits. Major lifestyle adjustments were necessary.

The lightning speed of rural grapevines contracted with the slow crawl of farmers in pick-up trucks inspecting bean fields. I discovered that we were known as "the silly city folk who paid too much for their little farm." Because I had grown up in a small town, I understood the reluctance to accept outsiders. Families often lived on the same property for generations. They knew the names of their mailman, school bus driver, and road commissioner. Waving to other drivers on rural roads was expected. So, I did my best to learn names and wave at everyone we met on the roads. It wouldn't happen overnight, but I resolved to change our reputation by becoming involved in our neighborhood and community once we were settled.

Living in the country limited restaurant choices. Our only option within fifteen miles of the farm was a small diner. They served up great blueberry pancakes, omelets, and coffee, but no sushi or pad Thai. And with three young children we couldn't afford eating out all the time anyway. It was time to expand my home-cooked menu options before my crew declared mutiny over cheese pizza and spaghetti dinners every night. So, I stumbled through new recipes while the farm cats gathered at the back door whenever the aroma of burning or questionable food wafted through the kitchen window. It took a few months, but my versions of chicken parmesan and beef teriyaki were pretty good. Even my free-spirit-career-self would have eaten them.

Rural life had its own style of adventure. I quickly realized that fact when we received a bovine emergency phone call from a neighbor one morning. Some calves had broken through a fence and were cavorting in the ditches and running across the road. I drove the van down the road, told the kids to stay inside, and listened as our neighbor told me what to do. When the young cows trotted our way, one broke free of the herd and headed straight for me. I found myself staring straight into a heifer's huge brown eyes. Spreading my arms slowly, I murmured "Git along, little doggie!" Honestly. That was all my brain could come up with. I was glad my neighbor didn't hear. But the cow froze. Maybe she heard my heart pounding like a jack hammer and knew I was a green horn. Instead of running over me, she obediently wheeled around and followed the others walking in single file back to the pasture. All were safe and accounted for. I gingerly stepped around her fresh steaming pile of manure and hopped back into the van. The neighbor waved a thank you as my kids cheered.

In addition to the often-needed practice of corralling escaped livestock, I noticed many country homes dried their clothes outside. Only one of our suburban neighbors had used her clothesline to air out small rugs. One morning, as we drove to town, Alex, Amie, and Hannah began giggling and could not stop. A laundry line at the farm we had just passed exhibited generously sized pairs of underwear and long johns flapping in the breeze. I gently chided the children and bit my lip to stop my own grin.

The amount of filthy clothes we generated on the farm was exponentially greater than our previous suburban loads. Road dust, creek mud, and grass stains clung tightly onto the fibers of our clothing at the end of each day. We were not alone in our dirt magnetism. Rural clotheslines set the stage for colorful shows on the roads we traveled. Brisk winds snapped sheets and blankets on one farm, while overalls danced on the lines at the next. Flowered housecoats and checkered work shirts made me ponder the lives of country folk who wore them.

Our industrial-sized washer and dryer handled our laundry valiantly. Every morning, I trudged down the shaky basement steps with an overflowing basket of grimy clothes, and each afternoon I climbed back up with clean fluffy ones. I had never really thought about the clothesline strung between several stout posts in our back yard until that trip to the grocery store. And a few days later, while cleaning an old basement shelf, I discovered an old coffee can with a curious handle. It was filled with wooden clothespins. My hand froze just before dumping it in the trash can. Maybe it was time to follow the lead of our new neighbors and dry our clothes using the sun and wind instead of spinning the electric meter.

I loaded the washing machine the following morning after breakfast. After the cycle completion buzzer sounded, I piled everything into a basket and lugged it up the stairs. Wet clothes were heavy. Stopping to catch my breath in the kitchen, I grabbed a drink of water. Then, while balancing the basket on my hip, I blocked Jack and Ellie's escape from the back door and walked into the early fall sunshine. The faded green maple leaves trembled in a light breeze.

The kids were busy drawing chalk stick figures and flowers on our cracked sidewalk. I had a few minutes before war broke out over colors, someone scraped their elbow, or Amie was scratched by one of the kittens again. I placed the basket onto the grass and hung the clothespin holder on the line within reach. It was a clever design: a metal hanger had been twisted into a hook and attached through holes in the side of the coffee can so I could slide it ahead of me as I worked.

After picking up a little t-shirt from the top of the pile, I paused. I had never hung laundry out before. Did I use separate pins for each item or overlap articles and economize on the pins? Not sure of the right way of doing it, I did a mix of both and figured all would eventually dry. As I worked my way down the line, I stopped occasionally to make sure there was no fighting or crying. Our clothesline had been purposely set up to catch the early morning sun and my skin felt nicely warmed. Robins sang in the old silver maples, and our barn swallows swooped about. Before I knew it, I was done.

I proudly looked back toward the house at the double rows of shirts, towels, and pants fluttering on the lines. Alex and Amie discovered the enticing wet clothes and ran shrieking underneath in an impromptu game of hide-n-seek. Hannah toddled over, then sat in the grass picking violets. I chased the big kids until we were all out of breath, then we all flopped down on our backs near Hannah and gazed skyward. I sighed with contentment and named cloud shapes with my children. The scent of freshly washed laundry enveloped us.

After lunch, I settled everyone down for naps and stepped outside to check on my project. The t-shirts felt dry, but towels and jeans were still damp. So, I lay down on a blanket under the maple tree and closed my eyes, luxuriating in a few peaceful moments. Clyde wandered over, lay beside me, and placed his golden head on my stomach. I stroked his soft fur and swatted a fly away. Lulled by the warm air, I closed my eyes. As the sun drifted westward, small voices from my bedroom window alerted me that everyone was awake. Clyde nudged my ribs to make sure I had heard. I stretched, yawned, and walked inside to retrieve my darlings. Our afternoon activity was a game of kickball in the front yard until Ellie ran off with the red rubber ball.

After we caught Ellie and put her back in the house with Jake, I checked the laundry. All the clothes were dry. I slowly worked my way along the lines, tossing each item into the basket and plinking clothes pins into the canister. I held a towel to my nose and inhaled its sweet smell. I carried the basket back inside for folding later and got everyone ready for a walk to the creek.

A new tradition was born after we joined the community clothesline show. It was another small step toward becoming an accepted part of our small town. My loss of undergarment privacy was far outweighed by the sheer joy of completing a job that used to be drudgery. I suddenly understood what our neighbors had known all along. Happiness could be found in even the simplest kinds of work. Hanging clothes on the line, serving a delicious (admittedly sometimes just edible) dinner to loved ones, and helping a neighbor round up cows were truly enjoyable tasks. I just needed to be open to the opportunities when they arose.

Chapter 6

THE TELEPHONE STARTLED ME AWAKE one afternoon. I had fallen asleep on the couch and scrambled over Clyde, Jake, and Ellie trying to answer before it woke the children. My foot landed on a sharp-edged plastic skid loader toy just as I reached the receiver. I cursed quietly and answered while hopping on one foot. My youngest brother and his family needed directions; they were coming to stay the weekend and explore our new place.

Curious friends and relatives wanted to witness our new lifestyle. The distraction was good because every day I discovered additional items for my "DIM" (Do It Myself) and "PRPH" (Projects Requiring Professional Help) lists. At least the "Potentially Deadly Hazards" list was dwindling. Hosting guests from Iowa, Wisconsin, Minnesota, Massachusetts, and Missouri made me forget the mountain of work I was facing for a little while.

We didn't worry about visitors being bored. Catching fireflies, wading in the creek, and roasting marshmallows over bonfires were great options. Watching thunderstorms sweep through the hills from our front porch was better entertainment than any movie theater offering.

The first ones to visit our farm was the young couple who had thrown our good-bye party. We proudly toured them around our little assortment of buildings and land. Later that evening we settled down for dinner, which featured an incredibly dry pot roast and slightly burnt potatoes. It wasn't one of my better efforts. I secretly fed mine to Jake under the table. After chasing the kids back to bed three times, the adults reminisced suburban adventures of cheering on the Chicago Bulls at the old stadium and riding wooden roller coasters at the amusement park. We laughed as quietly as we could, finished a bottle of wine around midnight, and all went to bed.

The house was silent for two hours. Then Hannah's screams pierced the dark. She was teething. I gave her some medicine, held her on the front porch until she stopped crying, then staggered back upstairs. Sixty minutes later she cried again. And ninety minutes after that. When my friend confided to me the next morning that she was pregnant with their first, I didn't know whether to offer congratulations or sympathy.

The playgroup moms drove out a few weeks later. It was wonderful to see their smiling faces as they tumbled out of their minivans; I had missed them immensely. After lots of hugs, we turned the children loose to play in the front yard while the moms caught up with each other's lives. Later that afternoon, Alex and Amie proudly led our group down to the pasture to see the cows and pick wildflowers. Afterwards, we paraded back to the house. Each family took turns in the pink tub while I made our traditional playgroup dinner: macaroni and cheese, green grapes, and hot dogs (I had that menu mastered).

Harvest machinery trundling up and down the road produced screams of excitement. Children raced to the picture window to watch balers, combines, and tractors rumble past. We settled the kids in the living room for a slumber party after story time; sleeping bags and small bodies lay scattered everywhere. Then the moms slipped out on the front porch to share a bottle of wine and memories. The next morning, a lump lodged in my throat as I helped the families pack back into their vehicles. Alex, Amie, Hannah, and I stood at the end of the lane, waving goodbye. I wondered if I would ever see those friends again.

Nights became cooler. It was time to prepare for winter, register Alex for preschool, and organize the rest of our house. The farm kitchen and pantry were fully functional after hosting all our guests. Since we were not sure how quickly our gravel road would be cleared of snow, I built up our inventory of pasta, canned vegetables (much to the disappointment of the kids), and ingredients for my signature dishes. Extra jars of peanut butter, jelly, and applesauce lined the pantry shelves, and spare loaves of bread filled the freezer.

Most of our furniture had found places to settle. I'd hung pictures and art on the plaster walls. Alex, Amie, and Hannah were prolific with crayons, so the refrigerator was well-decorated. Thankfully we didn't own much in the way of knickknacks, which was good with three wagging tails and three little kids ramming around.

I had haphazardly thrown clothing into dresser drawers after everyone chose their bedrooms. Our closets were tiny cubbyholes with narrow metal rods that only held a few hangers. Maybe previous occupants hadn't owned much clothing. The kids and I did. Culling was necessary. I started in my room, where all remains of my corporate life were tossed on the donation pile, along with one mini skirt that had squirreled itself between several pairs of jeans. I was a farm mom now and needed room for sturdy shirts and pants that would stand up to sorting piles of lumber, fixing pipes, and nailing boards into place. My free-spirit-career-self sighed and gave up encouraging me to hold onto remnants of my past life. Dance club days were past.

I followed the same process in the kid's rooms. Outgrown items went into the donation boxes unless they could be handed down. Almost all their clothes went into the dressers; easier for them to reach. Nicely pressed clothing certainly wasn't a high priority, as evidenced when the kids had unearthed my old iron during our final unpacking phase. Amie examined the appliance carefully, then asked me what it was. I grinned and placed it on a stack of things destined for the attic.

By far the largest category of things our family owned was toys. A bewildering jumble of wooden and plastic playthings littered every room of our farmhouse. Once a week, I conducted a weekly sweep to ensure there were still hardwood floors beneath the chaos. I knew early childhood wouldn't last forever, but having a house decorated in "Lego" style wasn't my ideal. Plus, I already had plenty of scars from tripping over miniature cars and dolls in the middle of the night. A method of toy storage was needed. Laundry baskets were the answer: they were cheap and easy to carry. One or two in each room did the trick. Every evening, before story time, we did a quick pick-up of playthings and tossed them into the baskets. Our floors were safer.

The final room to organize was our mud porch. It became home to all outerwear because jackets and shoes needed to be within easy reach when we raced out the back door. I lined the walls with hooks for coats and used more clothes baskets for shoe and boot storage. Solo shoes were given to the dogs, a very bad idea with obvious results.

Our house felt homier once everything had a place. The fact that we didn't have a large amount of storage space prevented us from falling into the fever of materialistic consumerism. My children became well accustomed to hearing the word "no" when they begged for something new. I simply reminded them their dressers and toy baskets were already overflowing. My favorite possession (besides dogs and kids) was the view from my front porch. Luckily it required no storage.

Clyde's Tortellini Chowder

1 sweet onion
2 jalepeno peppers
3 c. chicken broth
1 t. cumin
2 T. flour
2 T. butter

1 red pepper
2 large potatoes
2 c. frozen corn
2 c. ½ n ½
cheese tortellini, cooked

Cook onion, peppers (finely chopped) in a little butter until soft. Add cumin, broth and peeled cubed potatoes - cook until tender. Melt butter in small dish, add flour and stir into soup along with corn and ½ n ½. Cook until thickened, then add drained pasta.

Chapter 7

WHILE REACHING PAST THE APPLESAUCE for a box of pancake mix one morning, my arm bumped a jar. It teetered at the shelf's edge, and I caught it just before it crashed on the stairs. That would have made a nasty, time-consuming mess. Gazing at the label, I vaguely remembered my mother cooking Macintosh apples in the fall. She poured the mash into bags and froze them for use later.

Several days later, a new neighbor rescued me during our afternoon walk. Alex, in his yellow fireman's boots, had forged ahead with the wagon picking up stray ears of corn left by the combines. Clyde trailed him. I was pushing Amie and Hannah in the stroller when Jake and Ellie, who were tied to my waist, decided to head in opposite directions. The young woman laughingly helped untangle me from the leashes around my shins and introduced herself as a daughter of the family up the road. Her name was Becky. She commandeered the stroller while I concentrated on my disobedient canines. Becky explained that she was taking a break from picking apples at their farm. Her mother was in the kitchen cooking applesauce. The young girl invited us to come over and harvest as many apples as we wanted (it would save her some work)!

I thanked her for saving me and promised we would be over in an hour. Becky gave me directions and continued toward her home. The kids, dogs, and I turned around and trudged back uphill to our farm. After a quick lunch, I loaded the kids into the van along with a stack of paper grocery bags. It was a short drive, and I parked at the end of their lane near a white clapboard farmhouse. The massive apple tree in front of the house was so laden with fruit that the lower branches almost touched the ground. I released Alex, Amie, and Hannah from their car seats, and they jumped out with bags in hand. There were apples everywhere. Becky met us and climbed up a ladder set against the trunk, gently shaking limbs to send fresh ones showering down around us.

Real apple gathering was a new experience for me. I was used to glossy, red, perfectly shaped specimens stacked neatly in supermarket produce bins. These had spots, bumps, and bruises. I bit into one cautiously; the flesh was snowy white with the perfect amount of tartness-- just like the ones my mom had used for her applesauce. My kids helped for five minutes and then discovered a children's outdoor play set. Ditching their bags, they raced to the swings, teeter totter and slide. I kept picking while Becky pushed the girls on the teeter totter and Alex ran up and down the slide. After thirty minutes, I had four full sacks of apples.

My arms were tired and my back ached. Figuring we had more than we could eat, I loaded the heavy bags into the van. Terry, Becky's mother, came out to say hello and asked me what I planned to do with them. She smiled when I mumbled something about freezing them and offered to teach me how to can. I followed Terry into their cozy home which was filled with the heavenly aroma of cinnamon.

I watched Terry ladle cooked and mashed apples into sterilized jars, place a lid on top after wiping the rim, and twist a band over the lid to tighten it. Then she placed the jars in a boiling water bath to process. Just before the timer went off, my exhausted kids filed inside behind Becky.

We headed home for naptime after I stowed a borrowed pot, jars, lids, and written instructions next to the apples in the van.

With the kids tucked into their beds, I retreated to an old hammock under one of the maple trees with the instructions. The warm afternoon lulled me asleep, until a pesky fly buzzed around my nose. I swatted at it and stretched. Clyde's tail thumped on the ground. The apples were calling. I grabbed one of the bags, a paring knife, and two clean bowls. One bowl I filled with water to prevent the apple pieces from browning, and the other was for discards. I dragged everything out to the front porch and tied Jake and Ellie to posts so they could enjoy the late afternoon sunshine too.

After peeling and slicing half of the apples from that bag, my discards greatly outnumbered the good parts. Faced with the heap of skins, rotten parts, and cores, I sighed and realized that it was going to take longer than I thought. Forty more minutes netted me a pot full of acceptable material. Stepping carefully around my slumbering canines, I carried the scraps across the road and dumped them over the fence for the neighbor's Guernsey heifers. They trotted toward me and quickly devoured the treats.

Alex had already wandered downstairs when whimpers from Amie and Hannah signaled their naps were over too. Once everyone was seated at the table, I gave them cheese and crackers and stern instructions to stay clear of the stove. Then I put the pot of apples on a burner. The pieces simmered as I stirred, smashed, and sprinkled cinnamon sugar into the mix. The scent of cooking apples drifted outside, attracting our always hopeful farm cats to the back door.

Water in the borrowed pot boiled on an adjacent burner. I placed the jars and lids inside for the recommended time to sterilize them, then removed them to cool slightly. I herded the kids out to the living room and turned on the television just in case my virgin canning adventure went horribly awry. I'd heard stories of exploding jars that sent glass fragments through the air like missiles. Safety first.

Following Terry's example, I filled jars, placed lids on top and tightened everything down with rings. Scraps went into a bowl for our dinner; the barn cats finally gave up their pitiful mewing and wandered off to hunt mice. Working carefully, I lowered each jar into the kettle of boiling water, set the timer, and crossed my fingers. Then I went to the living room and wedged myself between Hannah, Alex, and Amie as they watched cartoons. When the timer buzzed, I trotted back to the steamy kitchen, removed the jars from the kettle with canning tongs, and turned off the burners. Six beautiful pints of homemade applesauce cooled on a towel.

The highlight of dinner that night was dessert. The kids proclaimed it to be the best applesauce they had ever tasted. Grinning while wiping their faces clean, I felt like a true farm girl. Five hours of hard work may have only netted me six dollars' worth of groceries, but I had learned how to preserve food for my family. The little influencer voice inside my head murmured its approval, while my single-career-self paused on her Tibetan expedition to simply shake her head.

Chapter 8

I TOOK THE LIST OF "Potential Deadly Hazards" off the refrigerator one morning after dropping Alex off at his new morning preschool. While the girls built a blanket fort in the living room, I sipped coffee and perused the items still needing to be addressed. Only a few issues remained on those scribbled yellow pages; it was time to address them.

As a child, I had admired my father's ability to fix things. I handed him tools and observed how he glued water pipes together and spliced electrical wires for new switches. I badgered him until he taught me some basic maintenance techniques. However, my talents leaned more toward artistic than mechanical. That fact did not prevent me from trying to fix toasters, doorknobs, and other miscellaneous things. I enjoyed "repairing" items that he quietly re-assembled correctly later.

My do-it-yourself activities had provided hearty entertainment for local hardware store employees in the suburbs. They probably drew straws to determine who helped me when I darkened their doorways with bags of parts. But they generously provided guidance without laughing and recommended professionals when safety was an issue. Despite their sage advice, I still had plenty of mishaps. The tinkle of breaking glass from my over-enthusiastic drilling while installing blinds on a pair of French doors still echoes through my mind whenever I grab a power screwdriver. The money saved by doing it myself did not begin to cover the replacement windows.

Plumbing projects were not my forte either. I was decent at fixing toilet flanges and faucet aerators, but the little plastic seals between pipes often leaked worse after I installed new ones. Hoping I'd have better luck on a larger scale issue, I tackled the foul-smelling sink hole that mysteriously appeared in our suburban back yard one day. I started excavating with a garden tool. The neighbors raced over when they looked out their kitchen window and could only see two legs protruding from a three-foot-wide hole. My torso dangled inside the pit as I scooped mud out with the hand trowel. The husband laughed, retrieved a couple of shovels from their garage and helped me dig. We quickly reached the source of the leak, a crack in the ancient clay sewer pipe. I proudly patched it with a substance I purchased from the helpful hardware guys the next day and filled dirt back into the hole—only to have a different soggy spot appear upstream three days later. The professional service man cleared tree roots from our sewer line the following week, shaking his head the entire time while side-stepping my dig site.

Despite past misadventures, I considered my hammers, wrenches, and screwdrivers dear friends. Acquiring new skills was not out of the question, as evidenced by my new canning proficiency and ability to herd livestock. The next project on the "Deadly Hazards" list was removing the tattered orange carpet runner on the steep steps leading to the second level of our grand old Victorian home. Tearing it out sounded like an easy, fun thing to do. I should have known better.

Once the kids were settled for naps the following afternoon, I knelt at the bottom landing and eyed my opponent. Prying a corner of the runner up, I coughed as the backing disintegrated to dust. The remaining strings of fiber lifted slightly, so I tugged harder. Nothing. I gave it a mighty heave. Suddenly it released and I flew backwards onto the hardwood floor grasping a two-inch section of disgusting nylon. After muttering a few not-very-nice-words, I picked myself up. Just like in a horror movie, the stairwell grew longer right before my eyes. It was time for reinforcements.

After rummaging through my tool chest, I pulled out a small hammer, knife, pliers, and gloves. Returning to my worksite, I stepped over all three dogs lounging on the dining room floor. It was tempting to stretch out on the sofa myself. With my noisy implements, I risked waking the children-- or maiming myself in the process. But I was determined to make progress on my project.

Donning gloves, I grasped a different corner of the carpet and scraped underneath with the screwdriver. It was easier with tools, but as I worked it became apparent that the carpet had been nailed, stapled, and glued. Once a small piece of carpet was removed, tiny nails and staples remained embedded in the wood. I had to pull each one out individually with the pliers. It took an hour to clear the first step. Black dust covered my face, hands, and arms. Voices echoed from the bedrooms; project time was over. I quickly washed up in the kitchen sink and ushered my darlings downstairs. After cookies and juice, we trooped outside to finish painting the small shed across the lane.

It took fourteen days to complete the stair runner demolition. My fingers, knuckles, and elbows were scraped and bruised. Both thumbs sported multiple comic strip bandages to protect deeper wounds. But the carpet was gone, adhesive scrubbed away, and nails were pulled. That left the bare wood exposed, which turned out to be even more treacherous than the old runner had been. Before someone ended up in the emergency room, I purchased simple pads on our next trip to town. Fastened with carpet tacks, they provided stable footing that didn't prevent the beautiful rosy wood from shining through.

We celebrated the completion of two projects (the stairs and shed) with a visit to our favorite park. Alex and Amie rang the red fire engine's brass bell while I pushed Hannah on a swing. Then I chased my kids around the playground until we collapsed at the picnic table with our cooler full of granola bars, cheese sticks, and juice boxes. Vivid scarlet and purple clouds stretched across the western sky as I drove my crew home. One by one the kids nodded off in their car seats. I was content. A good country life was possible. It just required learning new skills and balancing work with a healthy amount of play.

Chapter 9

JAKE TRIED TO ESCAPE the icy well water, but I held his collar firmly. Washing the green manure out of his thick coat with a garden hose was a challenge-- I got just as wet as he did. At least Ellie, his partner in crime, was merely muddy. After both were shampooed and sweeter smelling, I tied them to posts in the weak September sunshine. Our fenced yard in the suburbs, where the dogs and kids had romped without worry, was sorely missed. There was no safe containment on the farm.

A heavy wooden door separated the kitchen and mud porch. It did a decent job of keeping the dogs confined when it was shut tight. But my young children rarely closed doors. Jake and Ellie discovered the sagging storm door was easy to nudge open, granting them freedom to run. And both dogs excelled at slipping free of their collars as well, even when they were tied out. I was in a constant state of concern until the smelly and exhausted mongrels returned. At least the kids didn't have the same desire to escape. Yet.

One morning, as I raked rusty nails into a pile in the machine shed, I discovered a forgotten gift from one of my suburban friends. Faded wooden picket panels, posts, and a gate leaned against one of the heavy metal doors. They were the perfect amount for a dog run right outside the mud porch. It would keep my "mongrel Houdinis" safe and curtail the ulcer I was surely developing.

My brother Randy offered to help when I told him of my plan. It would prevent him from having to take everything apart and reassemble it like he had done with the bed frame I'd "put together" for Alex. Early one Saturday morning, my son and I gathered post-hole diggers, shovels, and trowels. Randy pulled into our lane with miscellaneous supplies in the back of his truck. I threw some warm cookies on a plate and delivered them to Amie and Hannah as they played with plastic construction tools on a blanket.

An unseasonably hot sun warmed our backs as Alex helped us lay out string for the enclosure boundaries. The kids captured the kittens who tried to bat our string and fed them bits of cookies. Randy and I began to dig holes for the posts. The first several were easy digging through rich loam and clay subsoil. No cement was necessary; posts were easily secured by packing dirt around them. It was near the crumbling sidewalk that the trouble began. About six inches down, our shovels bounced off an underground tangle of roots from that ancient maple tree. We used hand spades to chop through each woody extension, only to discover an additional layer underneath. Silence settled over the work site.

It took longer to dig that fourth posthole than it had for all the holes prior to it. With five more to go, we were too hot, sweaty, and frustrated to continue. We placed the rest of the project on hold for the following weekend. Blisters threatened to pop on my thumbs and my shoulders ached. Randy packed up his tools and left while the kids and I gathered on the couch for a movie. I fell asleep before they did.

The next weekend we started earlier. One of the posts required adjustment; the kids had crashed into it with a tricycle. My mind fast-forwarded to the future and envisioned those same driving skills behind an actual vehicle. While tamping extra dirt at the base, I made a mental note to purchase helmets before anyone received driving permits.

Once the final post was tamped into position, we moved the rest of the fencing materials down to our construction site. Each panel was attached to the posts with heavy screws that sank into the soft wood easily. The final piece was the gate. Finessing the hinges and lock to fit required a few heavy swings with the hammer to convince them to behave. The latch made a satisfying click when the bolt shot home. After we put our tools away, I gazed around at the finished product and smiled. The enclosure was perfect.

In eight days, Jake figured how to slip through the gate when the wind jiggled the latch loose. Ellie followed his lead. The kids' driving skills did not improve. After a few weeks, every post wobbled and the panels leaned in different directions. My dream of a functional picket fence to corral my wayward hounds was a disaster. As I filled the dishwasher one morning, I noticed the gate swinging open again. After wiping my hands dry, I read books to the kids on the front porch while we waited for our four-legged free spirits to find their way home.

Winter was quickly approaching, and I wanted to complete at least one more project before bitter weather chased us indoors. The problem was trying to figure out which one to tackle next. In addition to our home (which alone could have kept me occupied for the next twenty years), the farm had an early nineteenth century era wooden barn, two large metal sheds, and three small buildings.

The three-story barn's exterior was sided in white asbestos shingles that chose random times to fall off and shatter when they hit the ground. A solid iron framework climbed up inside the hurricane-resistant cement silo next to the barn. Two huge wooden sliding doors opened into the barn's middle floor. Stout wooden pegs held together the hand-hewn support posts and beams. A large opening on the south side was covered by a plastic tarp; at some point there had been another set of doors, but they were gone. On the lower level, rusted milking stanchions lined the cement troughs covered with a foot of ancient, dried manure.

The largest metal shed stood slightly behind the farmhouse on the north border of our property. One half of its interior was used to store large round hay bales for the cows who currently resided in the pasture. The other half was rented as storage for another neighbor's tractors and implements. It smelled of motor oil, grease, and potential dismemberments. I declared the building off limits to children (which meant they ran up there every time I was distracted.)

Three smaller structures lined the lane near the front of our property. Piles of construction materials rested haphazardly around all the foundations. Every exterior wooden surface cried for a coat of paint. Since organization was comforting to me when faced with an overwhelming amount of work, I decided to tackle the mountains of sharp-edged siding materials first.

After breakfast one Sunday, I hung the laundry while the kids blew bubbles for the kittens to chase. Once the last t-shirt was fluttering on the line, I approached a pile of metal near the old milk shed. In between checking on the kids every few minutes, I separated pieces according to shape and swept them clean. Then I dragged each length into the lower level of the barn and stacked them on racks above the old, rusted milking stanchions. After the kittens ran away to find their mother, Alex, Amie, and Hannah began riding their plastic vehicles on our driveway. I finished the pile of siding just in time to break up a fight over whose turn it was to drive the prized yellow coupe. Playing traffic cop, I noticed how much the kids struggled to roll wheels through the gravel. Suddenly, an idea struck me.

Our brood had spent many happy hours racing their little fleet on our suburban home's smooth black top driveway. Paving our farm lane was cost-prohibitive, but we had a huge three-story barn just waiting to be used. The barn's middle level was an open area, with building supplies left from the previous owners stacked against its walls. It was perfect for an indoor play spot with plenty of room to zoom around on small vehicles. There was even enough space to give our refrigerator-box playhouse a permanent home instead of it squatting in the living room gathering dust bunnies.

I started my barn project the next afternoon, using the baby monitor to alert me when the kids woke from their naps. First, I cordoned off stacks of wood and supplies in the shop area with a bright orange plastic snow fence. Clyde joined me as I cleaned, sniffing out old raccoon scat in the corners. Our magnetic sweeper picked up stray nails. Then, armed with gloves and rakes, I gathered moldy hay and bat guano into heaps. After shoveling those piles into a wheelbarrow, I dumped the foul-smelling stuff into the cattle yard. Long wooden panels nailed across the tarp stretched over the open gap on the south end provided a safer, more solid barrier.

I drew chalk highway lines on the ancient barn floor timbers, made road signs using cardboard and construction paper, and placed the playhouse on an old piece of carpet at the intersection of Main and Broadway. All our plastic vehicles were parked in spaces at the imaginary grocery store lot, just waiting to be driven. I even lugged the basket of Alex's metal tractor toys up to the barn, imagining our Victorian house's woodwork exhaling with relief. The loads of corn and soybeans gleaned from the road on our walks went into a plastic pool; just waiting for the little tractors and wagons to move them around. Our resident mice must have excitedly rubbed their tiny paws together at the unexpected winter feast laid before them. We had already done the work for them.

Barn Town was ready. One blustery afternoon I led Alex, Amie, and Hannah up to the middle level and proudly slid the big doors open. Their delighted expressions were worth every drop of sweat I had put into the task. Hannah immediately dragged her blanket inside the cardboard house and played peek-a-boo through the cut-out windows as Amie and Alex rocketed around on their vehicles. And after a few crashes, the kids learned that those barn timbers didn't budge an inch. Unlike the picket fence.

Barn town was a huge success. I kept a box of band aids in the workshop to cover occasional mishaps and organized the workshop area while the kids occupied themselves. We often brought Jake, Ellie, and Clyde with us. If I remembered to shut the doors securely, everyone was able to run freely. With the wise words of our new pediatrician "relax and enjoy your children" ringing in my ears, sometimes I just sat with my back against a timber and threw tennis balls for the dogs while watching Alex, Amie, and Hannah play. I was truly grateful to be a mother.

The more time we spent in the barn, the more I realized how amazing that structure was. An old hay hook hung from the rafters; the space must have smelled wonderful when the mow was filled with alfalfa hay and the loft held harvested grain. I yearned for a written history from previous occupants but hadn't unearthed any records hidden away. At least the barn had a useful role once more instead of just sitting sad and empty. The kids and dogs loved it.

Late one evening, I took down the yellow pages of project lists hanging on the refrigerator. With a little bit of elbow grease and minimal cost, our stairs were safer, the machine shed had a new roof panel, dangerous metal siding had been stored securely, and the kids had a wonderful indoor play area. But most of the remaining items required money. While sipping a glass of merlot, I drew up balance sheets with our current financial information. Then, next to each DIM (Do It Myself) and PRPH (Projects Requiring Professional Help) goal, a ballpark estimate of how much they might cost was scribbled. I looked at the results, sighed, and poured another glass of wine. Our family had moved into a country money abyss.

# Chapter 10

A COLD WIND RUSTLED THE WITHERED corn stalks in the field across the road. They marched in rows like hunched old men. I stood barefoot beneath the silver maple in our front yard. Its yellow leaves littered the thin green grass.

He looked around the buildings and gardens after slamming the trunk down. "You'll never make it out here on your own." he said and climbed into the car.

Slowly I walked to the front porch and sat heavily on the bottom step. Cartoon laughter from the living room television drifted through the screen door. My three children giggled, oblivious. I was now a single mom living on a small farm in the middle of nowhere. Following my dream of living in rural America had taken my life down an unexpected path.

The next day, I resolutely drove to town for an important errand. I parked in front of a jewelry store and took some deep breaths. A small bell tinkled as I opened the door. I explained my situation to an elegantly dressed man, whose hand reached out to take the rings and necklace. I dropped them one by one into his palm, hoping they would bring some desperately needed cash. Jewelry could not keep me warm like a pair of insulated coveralls. After the man counted out a small stack of bills on the counter, I grabbed the money and fled the jewelry store before my tears escaped. Brisk autumn air helped me recapture control as I drove to the farm supply and clothing store. I bought my coveralls and a giant bag of dog kibble.

Bleak finances were not going to stand in the way of my dream. Frugal living newsletters introduced me to a wealth of ideas on how to save money. Low-cost meals and thrift stores kept us fed and clothed, except for a few items like the insulated coveralls for me and warm boots for the kids. I was very thankful we were all healthy.

Using our clothesline instead of the dryer decreased one utility bill. Another way to save money was how we handled our trash. We had paid a monthly fee in the suburbs to have it hauled away. It was different in the country. A local service would happily pick our bags up and add it to the local landfill for a fee. Or we could incinerate on our own property like our neighbors. Fire was free.

Burning was not a new concept for us. Backyard bonfires had already become a beloved tradition. At least once a week, weather permitting, Alex and I arranged twigs and rolled newspapers beneath logs inside a dirt ring encircled by lawn chairs. Once the fire was crackling, we dug into the wicker basket filled with provisions for s'mores. Clyde, Jake, and Ellie happily cleaned up any spills. I adored having all three kids cuddle close on those evenings, even if they were rather sticky. Owls and coyotes occasionally joined the night symphony as we picked out constellations in the velvet sky. When I tucked my brood into their beds, the lingering sweet scent of wood smoke made me smile.

There was nothing sweet about incinerating trash. My brother delivered an empty metal barrel to the farm, and punched holes through the sides for ventilation. We set it up on an old foundation behind the house. Alex and I tugged grapevines from the cement cracks and scraped matted grass off the surface until we had a reasonably clear zone that wouldn't allow flames to spread. Instead of a bonfire one evening, we dragged several of our stockpiled moving boxes to the barrel and held a ceremonial burning. Alex's eyes lit up as he helped stoke the fire. The girls watched from a distance. Glowing bits of paper twirled above our heads and faded as they drifted away. Embers that reached the ground were quickly stomped out.

From that evening on, whenever we had enough burnable material, I stationed myself near the barrel in my new coveralls to monitor the small blaze. Stars winked down at me as if they were enjoying the warmth as well. Just like laundry, dealing with trash became another pleasurable activity instead of a dreaded chore.

Controlling vegetation was another rural use of fire. Weeds flourished along fence lines; spring burning of the land beneath them was an accepted way to keep them clear. Fires were also used to re-establish prairie areas, mimicking on a smaller scale the huge blazes that had swept through the plains long ago.

Alex and I decided to burn our overgrown ditch one day. Without any guidance, I helped him strike matches and light the matted brown grass. It caught quickly. The flames followed our intended course, and everything was going well until the wind shifted. In seconds, the fire breached our squirt gun containment strategy. There was no time to get a shovel or hoe, so we quickly stomped at the flames with our boots. Thankfully the wind switched direction again, and we regained control before our rubber boots burned through. After that experience, I consulted with our neighbors before any major fire undertakings. We didn't need to fuel the country grapevine with our lack of common sense. And the volunteer fire department was busy enough.

Harnessing a basic element of the earth to maintain land and dispose of paper waste saved us money and provided hours of entertainment. But no matter how frugally we lived, our savings dwindled quickly. Expensive winter heating bills, foreshadowed by frost and mist lingering over low areas in the morning, were imminent. Clouds transformed from wispy white puffs to heavy purple and grey rows. Withered yellow leaves released their hold from our silver maples, drifted to the ground, and were swept away by the cold winds.

Alex adjusted nicely to his preschool morning program. After we dropped him off, the girls and I returned to the farm. They played in the barn while I pounded nails into loose siding panels and caulked windows and worked on simple DIM projects. After we picked Alex up at noon, we headed back home for lunch and nap time.

Heavier jackets, hats, and gloves were necessary for our daily walks after lunch. Most of our neighborhood's fields had been harvested. On our hikes to the creek, we saw additional signs of winter's approach. Milkweed pods burst open, releasing strands of silky seeds to the air. Thistles bowed their faded purple heads away from the cold, leaden skies. Birds gathered into flocks, swooping low toward the earth and then back up into trees where they noisily chattered.

Rainy fall days were perfect for painting the drab bedroom walls that had been hiding behind stacks of moving boxes. I wrangled some money from our clothing budget for paint and brushes. Alex chose sky blue for his room and tractor material for curtains. I set up my sewing machine in the dining room to stitch his window coverings together; it was less expensive than purchasing ready-made ones.

For the girls' shared bedroom, we sifted through at least one hundred color swatches before they agreed on a soft lilac. It accented the airy lace panels already hanging from their windows. After the walls were coated, I touched up a few splatters of violet on the white windowpanes—I was not the neatest painter—and discovered the sills had swollen shut from years of rain and snow. After a lot of scraping and tugging, I managed to open two of the three windows. Replacing them became high priority on the "Projects Requiring Professional Help" list.

At one time, the large room Amie and Hannah shared had been divided. The ghost of a plaster dividing wall was still visible from floor to ceiling. I'd seen a similar scar masked by a painted tree trunk in a home magazine. So, we used textured paint to make our tree feel like real bark, with limbs stretching across the walls. The girls and I spent many enjoyable afternoons adding leaves, dragonflies, ladybugs, and sunflowers to the mural. When it was too cold for Barn Town, we hauled toys to their room and played beneath that beautiful tree.

Despite my growing love for our country life, I spent a fair amount of time worrying. My brain dwelled on a million potential problems that could surface at any time. What would happen if one of the kids came down with a severe disease requiring serious medical care? How would we buy a new vehicle if the van broke down? What if the barn roof blew away in a windstorm? I briefly contemplated opening a bed and breakfast to make money. But who was willing to pay for a stay in a home where dogs howled, children whined, and the shrill alarm of the smoke detector signaled yet another blackened dinner?

Thankfully an unexpected income opportunity knocked one day during a conversation with my father. He was selling his second health food store, a sister business to the one my brother owned. A part-time employee was willing to cover three days a week; I could manage it the other days. The first time I opened the store's front door, the familiar metallic tang of vitamins tickled my nose. It smelled like home. That little voice inside my head whispered its approval of the new venture, but my free-spirt-career self was unable to communicate from the mountains of Patagonia.

Running a small business was a stark contrast from the research responsibilities of my past. Then, corporate officers had dictated every goal. As a sole proprietor, I controlled my own destiny. My pharmacy background helped establish an edge over our competitors, while re-entry into the work force refreshed me from the daily grind of childrearing and farm maintenance. I reacquainted myself with a nutritional approach to health issues and researched interactions between supplements and prescription drugs to ensure we made safe recommendations for our clients. Another benefit to my returning to work was our discovery of a wonderful babysitter who ran a day care in our small town. Alex, Amie, and Hannah enjoyed playing with other children under her watchful eyes; my kids were probably safer there than on our farm.

Happy customers spread the word about my expertise. Sales steadily increased. On weekends, the store became a family project. I set up displays or rearranged merchandise. Alex, Amie, and Hannah priced products and stocked shelves just like I had in my youth. But for some reason, I remembered working all day, whereas my three toiled for fifteen minutes, then chased each other with shopping carts or played cash register and moved items to different places. I kept reminding myself it was a good learning experience for them.

Several physicians in the area were interested in combining modern medicine with a holistic approach. They invited me to present information at health seminars sponsored by various organizations. To make my slides interesting and entertaining, I dressed the kids up in my old lab coats one day. Giving Alex, Amie, and Hannah props and directions, I snapped pictures as they pretended to be doctors and nurses with kittens and dogs as their patients. Our reputation for knowledgeable and ethical advice grew.

Returning to my health food store roots felt right and helped me become more health-conscious of my family's habits. I found better ways to camouflage vegetables for my picky eaters and made sure everyone received plenty of exercise. We took vitamins every morning. The health food store income wasn't going to transform us into millionaires, but it allowed us to purchase decent health insurance, fund occasional pizza nights, and start saving toward future expenses.

Chapter 11

EVEN THE WHIRLWIND COMBINATION of running a small business, raising children, and preventing our buildings from self-destruction could not disguise the fact that the days were shorter and darker. My seasonal sadness began to settle in. There were no suburban playgroup sessions to pull me out of it. Then Terry, Becky's mom, suggested that a few of us get together to make simple crafts once a week; I clutched at the idea like a drowning rat reaching for a stick.

When Terry, Becky, and another neighbor Jody arrived to make Halloween baskets one blustery evening, I was dodging splashes from three sudsy kids playing in the pink cast iron tub. Becky relieved me from my station, shielding her face with a towel. The adults escaped up to our big white barn, carrying an assortment of empty produce cans. Clouds raced across the sky, allowing glimmers of a full moon to shine through the breaks. I flipped on the lights after dragging the big sliding doors open, pushing hard to fight the wind.

Newspapers fluttered beneath cans of spray paint on a table I had set up in the workshop. I was grateful for my heavy sweatshirt; it was chilly even after the doors were closed. In the dim glow of flickering fluorescent bulbs, Terry showed us how to cover the tin cans with thin layers of white spray paint. We all took turns shaking the aerosols vigorously to keep warm. Luckily the barn was so drafty that it prevented the toxic fumes from overcoming us.

Once the base coats were dry, we punched two holes near the top rim with a hammer and nail for a wire handle. Then we cleaned up our workspace and transported the cans back down to the house. There, we set them up on the dining room table I'd recently picked up at a garage sale. It was a bit wobbly, but functional.

I helped Becky wrestle clean kids into their fuzzy pajamas. Then they all climbed onto the couch with books. Becky hoisted Hannah onto her lap as Alex and Amie settled themselves on either side to listen and help turn the pages. After kissing the tops of their damp heads, the sweet scent of baby shampoo lingered in my nose as I returned to the dining room.

Jody and Terry were painting details on their cans. Black cats and spider webs found their way onto mine. Terry wrapped floral wire around a pencil, threaded the ends through the holes punched at the top of her can, and formed it into a handle. Jody and I followed suit, although mine ended up rather lopsided. A final light coat of tan paint made them appear old. I designated mine as our new candy basket. Bidding good night to my friends' smiling faces, I slipped a ten-dollar bill into Becky's hand. It had been a good evening.

The following week we met at Terry's house to discuss ideas for our next project. Jody and I leafed through craft books, but many of the projects were intimidating. Then Terry found a pattern for "Quiet Books," a soft volume of cloth pages that offered activities like shape matching and counting for young children. I envisioned hours of peace and quiet. Then I realized that my brood's sharing capacity on a scale of 1-10 was a minus 5. One quiet book would lead to a third world war. I needed to make three. Jodi scribbled down how much fabric and notions were required for the project; I tripled the amounts. It was a good thing our health food store was doing well.

I spent an enjoyable hour wandering the aisles of the colorful fabric store one Sunday afternoon, enveloped in the textures and prints of woven cottons and polyesters. For Alex's book cover, I found farm implement material in gold and green. Hannah's binding would feature a peaceful rural scene, almost identical to her beloved blanket. I also purchased large amounts of felt buttons, snaps, and interfacing. Then I dug through my old sewing supplies until I found remnants of the material I'd used for crib pads. Cute black and white cows, accented in primary colors, would be Amie's book cover.

Cold November rains comingled with occasional snow flurries. I had less than two months to complete the quiet books. Terry held weekly evening work sessions at her house while Becky watched the kids at my farm. Tracing and cutting out shapes were the first steps. I beheaded my little ladybugs the first time around but was more careful with the scissors from then on. We took turns pressing interfacing on the different shapes. Hand-sewing snaps, sticky tape, and buttons onto the features was particularly challenging for me. I was relieved when we moved on to the assembling phase. A mother ladybug stored her babies inside a zippered pouch on one page while flowers snapped onto green stems on the next. Those joined other sorting and counting options inside the colorful clothbound cover.

As the books solidified, so did our friendships. We shared stories from our lives as we sewed, cut, and glued. Listening to the challenges Terry and Jody faced gave me a very different perspective on parenthood: their kids were finishing high school while mine were still drinking from sippy cups. I was swimming through the murky water of early childhood without any grandmotherly guidance and found their seasoned advice reassuring.

It had become apparent during quiet book construction that my Victorian home lacked insulation. As I stitched pages together beneath the dim light of our dining room chandelier (three books required extra nights beyond our gatherings at Terry's house), I worked with a blanket around my shoulders. Wearing thin gloves kept my hands from freezing, but I stopped that after sewing a thumb onto Alex's cover. The mistake required a precious extra hour to fix.

Clyde, Jake, and Ellie had grown into their winter coats. I envied them. The kids and I dressed in triple layers and double socks. The old furnace groaned as it sent up small puffs of warm air through the vents. I could almost see the dollars wafting up through the tall ceilings into the un-insulated attic. As further proof of how drafty our home was, Amie and Hannah entertained themselves by scratching designs in the delicate frost on the INSIDE of our living room windows.

When we ran errands in town, we luxuriated in the free heat of big box stores. I stumbled onto flannel sheets one day and splurged on a set for everyone. Extra blankets too. Area rugs and hallway runners helped us warm up as we hopped from one to another, avoiding the cold floors.

I tried to seal our leaky windows with plastic, but the wind simply swirled through it. Caulking was my next option, and it was one task that I knew how to do well. I emptied five tubes in the downstairs rooms alone, filling every cold crack I found. It helped slow the wind tunnel effect a little. And left my hands very sticky until the silicone on my fingers finally wore away.

One night, during my midnight trip to the bathroom and its wickedly frigid toilet seat, I felt an icy breeze outside the attic door. At the same time, my foot landed on a tiny metal car that had evaded our evening toy sweep. I limped to the toilet, sat down, and discovered only two squares remaining on the paper roll. Not my finest hour. After I crawled back between my flannel sheets, I made a mental note to investigate the attic in the morning.

The next day, while the kids drowned pancakes in maple syrup, I walked upstairs and cautiously opened the attic door. Cold air whistled past me; I had forgotten to shut the heavy panel that prevented heat from escaping through the eaves. Rolling my eyes, I grabbed a box of things I had been meaning to stow up there anyway and climbed the stairs. At the top, I noticed several white mounds near the attic windows. Picking up a broom, I cautiously prodded the unknown mass. If I required any more evidence that we were living in an economic black hole, I needed to look no further. The mounds were snow drifts blown in through the window frames.

I scooped the snow into a bucket with a dustpan, hauled it downstairs, and threw it out the back door. Those gaps went way beyond my caulking abilities. Then I remembered seeing some stray pieces of insulation in the basement. I retrieved them, raced back up to the attic and stuffed them into the crevices. When I stood admire my work, my head smacked into a wooden cross beam. Stars circled my head, and I sat down heavily. After the darkness cleared, I looked up. It wasn't normal for attic supports to bow downward. Apparently, we needed a new roof as well as new windows.

Despite the adverse conditions in our house, I completed all three quiet books just in time for Christmas Eve. After an afternoon of sledding down the barn hill in fresh powder, we drank hot chocolate and ate sugar cookies heavily decorated with frosting and sprinkles. When evening drew near, I dragged our potted evergreen from the front porch into the living room. It was a tradition we had started in the suburbs because I was always saddened at the number of unclaimed pines in tree lots after the holidays. We brought our live tree inside for one night, decorated it, and then planted it outside on Christmas day.

Alex, Amie, and Hannah festooned the small fir with handmade paper snowflakes and ornaments. Then I wove a string of twinkling white lights gently around it. Brightly wrapped presents were placed near its metal bucket. Finally, the kids were allowed to open one present before racing to bed in sleepless, sugar-laced, eager anticipation of Christmas dawn.

The kids rattled boxes, puzzling over which present to open. I placed identical packages in their small hands instead. Shiny paper shreds flew everywhere, and a bow landed on Jake's head. When the kids pulled their gifts from the boxes, the rapt looks on Alex, Amie, and Hannah's faces made every needle stick and snap battle worthwhile.

The quiet books went everywhere with the kids. My hand-made gifts did not necessarily buy hours of peace or quell heated arguments over whose fruit snack package contained the most purple dinosaurs, but sometimes ten minutes of silence was just enough to save the sanity of one mother's mind. And the best present I received that year was the social support and motherly guidance from my new rural friends.

Chapter 12

IN THE SUBURBS, WE NEVER QUESTIONED where our water came from. It was always clear and appeared with the simple twist of a faucet. An entire city department worked tirelessly to deliver safe drinkable liquid to each house via miles and miles of underground pipes. Our only responsibility was to pay the monthly bill on time. In contrast, the farm's water system was totally independent, drawing water from a mysterious network of underground aquafers. It was a little more complicated (an absolute understatement).

Our rural well, pump, and holding tank were housed in a dank underground room beneath what used to be the milk pump shed for the dairy operation. A heavy cement lid covered the port-hole entrance, which was just large enough to allow a person to pass through. I occasionally tugged the cover aside to peer down into the dim chamber, where a maze of old steel pipes exited a huge blue holding tank and headed in different directions to supply the house and buildings. Sometimes the pump made a soft thud or click when the lid was open, but the system functioned perfectly until one winter morning.

I awoke before the kids and shuffled to the bathroom in my slippers and heavy robe. It was cold. I flipped the light switch on and walked over to the sink to splash icy water on my face. But the only thing I received when I turned the knob was a hissing blast of air. Puzzled, I headed downstairs to try the kitchen faucet. Nothing there either.

The refrigerator light greeted me when I opened the door to grab a carton of milk. So, we had power. But no water for coffee. I stirred instant into a mug of milk and wracked my brain for ideas. I remembered solving one frozen pipe in our suburban house with a blow dryer; we had been on vacation and forgot to turn the heat on. Maybe it was as simple as that. Our basement was the same temperature as our refrigerator. But a bad feeling settled in my stomach, and it wasn't just because I was hungry.

I trudged downstairs to our gloomy basement. There were lots of pipes down there. Figuring the ones nearest the outside wall were most suspect, I grasped one with my right hand. It was chilly, but my skin didn't stick to it. Spider webs hanging near the wall caught me as I reached for another pipe. Cold but not frozen. Pulling sticky stuff from my fingers as I returned to the kitchen, I sipped my coffee milk shake and pondered the next step. The clock on the wall told me it was early, but not too early. Florida was an hour ahead. I called my father who had already gone for a balmy walk and eaten breakfast. He listened to my panicked description of our predicament and asked several questions. Decades of dealing with temperamental rural plumbing systems had given him plenty of experience with water woes. He thought the most likely culprit was a frozen holding tank.

I tiptoed to each child's bedroom door and heard only the soft breathing of deep sleep. Jake and Ellie snored on my bed. Avoiding the creaky step on the stairs, I padded into the mud porch. After tugging on boots, gloves, and a heavy coat, I walked to the well pit with Clyde at my side. Grunting and muttering some choice words, I heaved the sodden straw bales used for insulation over the lid aside. Then I wrestled the lid open and peeked down. The large, blue holding tank sported a heavy coat of white frost. That was different from previous well pit checks. I wasn't about to put a bare finger on the metal to test it.

I dragged the lid back into place, grabbed the keys to the van, and started the engine. Taking Alex to preschool a little early would allow us to use the school's indoor plumbing. As I trudged back to the house, Clyde trotted ahead and reached the back door before me, eager to get out of the wind. I headed upstairs to wake everyone. Alex dressed quickly while I pulled coats over the girls' pajamas. Grabbing granola bars from the cabinet on my way out, I buckled everyone into their car seats and handed out breakfast. At least the van was toasty.

We navigated the quiet back roads and parked in front of the squat brick building of the school, I stopped to ask the office secretary if we could use their bathroom, explaining what had happened. She nodded sympathetically. Frozen pipes and holding tanks were no surprise to anyone living in the country. I thanked her, holding Amie's little fingers in one hand as Hannah rode my hip. Alex's teacher had arrived early and grabbed a book to read to him until class began.

After the girls and I returned home, Amie and Hannah camped on the couch under a mound of blankets with Jake and Ellie to watch a movie. I trudged back outside to meet the enemy face to face. Never having ventured inside the well pit before, I armed myself with a flashlight and wrestled the lid open again. Even in daylight, the small room seemed menacing. Tugging my knit hat down over my ears, I lowered myself toward the dirt floor, using pipes as footholds.

The flashlight's dull yellow rays barely illuminated the tight space, which was mostly occupied by the giant holding tank. A small hole in the ceiling led to the interior of the shed above. I knew there was an outlet up there; snaking an extension cord through the hole would access power.

Warming the tank with a blow dryer might take days: I was not going to stay in what felt like a tomb for that long. But if I blasted the tank and pipes with a propane heater, I risked cracking them. Clyde's nose appeared at the pit opening. Climbing partially out, I reached up to pet him and breathe some fresh air.

Suddenly I remembered the electric heater I'd recently purchased for the bathroom. It was the perfect size. I went back down and spied some cement blocks in a corner. By moving them closer to the holding tank, they formed a perfect platform. The last thing I needed was an extension cord. I climbed back up and pulled myself out through the opening. The brisk wind was a welcome alternative to the stuffy space. I returned to the house and peeked into the living room. Amie was showing Hannah the photo album from our old house.

I snatched the heater from the bathroom and ran up to the barn to search for extension cords. Finding several candidates in the recently organized drawers, I lugged everything back into the well pit. The first cord was too short to snake through the hole. The longer one worked. After setting the heater up on the blocks and plugging it into the extension cord, I climbed out of the pit and scurried into the shed. But the cord wouldn't plug into the outlet without an electrical adapter.

I returned to the barn and rummaged around until I found an adapter behind some stray wiring. With the heater finally connected to power, I descended into the pit again, cranked the thermostat to high and was relieved to see the little coils behind its grate glow red. I checked everything one last time before forcing my arms to pull me up and out. After replacing the lid, I ran back inside the house to make real hot chocolate with milk since we still had no running water. Amie and Hannah declared it much better.

The girls and I picked Alex up from preschool at noon, used their bathrooms again, and returned home. We picnicked in the living room for lunch. The dogs circled in search of unguarded sandwiches and potato chips, nosing the carpet for crumbs. Ellie managed to grab my crust, and Jake scored the remnants of Amie's chips. Relieved that it was nap time, I settled the kids in their beds upstairs. Then I picked up our plates and cups and added them to the stack of unwashed dishes in the kitchen sink. I was exhausted and curled up beneath a blanket on the couch. Outside, a parade of neon orange-clad huntsmen sped up and down our road; their truck engines rattled the living room window. It was the first weekend of deer hunting season and you could almost smell the testosterone in the air. I fell asleep within minutes.

Jake's heavy panting woke me with a start. Shots echoed nearby. All three dogs paced nervously and followed me into the kitchen where I tried the kitchen faucet for the fiftieth time. It sputtered, groaned, and rewarded me with the blissful sound of liquid splashing into a glass.

Alex, Amie, and Hannah shuffled downstairs from their naps. After settling them at the table with snacks and modeling clay and hoping they didn't confuse the two, I bundled up one more time and returned to the pit. The frost on the holding tank had disappeared, so I climbed down, turned the heat setting to a low setting and checked connections to make sure everything looked good. Using the pipes as footholds worried me; I would add a note to buy a short stepladder to my to-do list. Then I climbed back up to the fresh air, patted Clyde's nose, secured the lid, and returned the sodden straw bales to their places. Grinning defiantly at the grey sky, I let out a joyful whoop. I had won my first skirmish in what would become a never-ending feud with the well pit.

Chapter 13

AS I POUNDED THE LAST NAIL into the loose barn board, I nipped the tip of my thumb through my thick gloves with the hammer. It stung. Cursing softly while shaking my hand, I tugged at the board. The old wood wiggled a bit, but it seemed to hold tight enough. After tossing the hammer and box of nails back into the tool bucket, I headed to the house. Grey clouds hovered low on the horizon.

We were ready for winter. The pantry bulged with food, I'd managed enough money to fill our propane tank, and we had enough toilet paper to survive any storm that left our gravel road unpassable for a few days. Water flowed freely into the house with the electric heater set on low in the well pit.

It was too cold to hang out in the barn, so I brought fresh toys down from the attic. While the kids were occupied, I focused on my promise to the huge cottonwood tree near the creek and considered uses for our twenty acres. The land needed help. The only vegetation that survived the cow's voracious appetites were twisted hawthorns, stunted crab apples, thistles, and wild roses. Mosquito-ridden swampy areas pocked with cloven hoof prints lay along shallower banks of the little waterway. Pasture rental income wasn't worth the devastation.

Our undulating acreage was unsuitable for traditional grain crops. The soil would just erode toward the creek. Terracing would correct that, but we didn't have a tractor or plow. It would take years of shoveling to reach the rich soil beneath the tangled weeds. One idea popped out among the brochures I'd gathered from the county soil and water conservation office: growing grapes for the wine industry of Illinois. The idea sounded incredibly romantic until I learned it would be very labor intensive. Determining an area with the necessary amount of sun exposure and equipment to plant and care for the vines as well as providing protection from ravenous deer and rabbits were just some of the daunting necessities. That idea was shelved after consuming some excellent cabernet, purely for research purposes.

One of our well-meaning friends recommended raising goats. We had plenty of room in the barn to re-establish a milking operation and could manufacture our own cheese and soap. I tried to imagine all of us cheerfully strolling outside every morning and night to do chores. But I had a feeling our brood would bear little resemblance to charming stories where everyone eagerly pitched in to help. Our book's title was more likely to be "Drafty House on Burdock Acres," starring one snarling mother and three whining children who didn't want to pull weeds or tend smelly animals.

A crop rotation program sponsored by the federal government appeared to be the best option for returning the land to a more natural state. It was part of the effort to restore Illinois waterways. Trees and shrubs, a riparian buffer, would form a protective filtration strip to reduce the amount of farm chemicals and soil reaching streams and creeks. We would be responsible for the cost of shrubs and seedlings, but the Department of Natural Resources would plant them.

The first step was to have the land surveyed and soil sampled. The forestry contract required separation from livestock; otherwise, the young plants would just be eaten. We decided to fence a large paddock around the cattle shed, just in case we decided on a herd of our own someday. Several fencing companies gave us estimates for barbed wire (ouch), wood (too expensive), and high tensile wire (just right so we hired them). We ordered trees from the Soil and Water Conservation sale. Work would begin in the spring.

Sometime in February, seed catalogs appeared in our dusty mailbox by the road. Now that we had a plan for the pasture, I switched my focus to gardening. We had cultivated a small plot in the suburbs, but its main contribution to the local ecosystem had been to fatten wild rabbits. Our neighbor's garden directly across the fence had flourished under their diligent care, but they were retired. Having babies had left me little energy for horticulture. We would have perished from starvation if not for the local grocer. I envisioned a different scenario in the country. Sun-drenched vegetables would help stretch our food budget and give me the digging-in-the-dirt-fresh-air therapy I needed to survive parenthood.

Once the ground thawed enough to work, our fence construction company arrived with equipment and supplies. I found myself lusting after their green tractor. Its engine-driven auger dug all the holes in about an hour. A stark contrast to several full days Randy and I had wasted manually digging one tenth the number of post holes for my disastrous picket fence. After the oak posts were set, wires were attached with staples and insulators and run the perimeter of the paddock. Our neighbors' cows were unhappy about the smaller area and added extra manure to the shed to show their displeasure.

We eagerly awaited arrival of the six hundred trees and shrubs we had ordered. The call for pick-up came one cold April morning. I worried all those plants would overwhelm our little pick-up, but thirty bags of bare root saplings did not require much space at all. I clucked over them like a mother hen after we stored them in a shed, keeping the roots moist until the forestry equipment arrived. When the weather forecast finally showed a clear window, a seedling planter and tractor were delivered.

The planting progressed quickly, except when their tractor became stuck in the thick mud on the other side of the creek. We called Terry's husband, Ken, who promptly rumbled over on his ancient but more powerful John Deere and pulled them out. The kids and I carried cookies down to the forestry men and watched them while they worked. It only took three days to sink the young trees and shrubs into the earth with the automated planter; it would have taken me a year on my own. When I walked down to inspect their work, I squinted mightily until I finally spotted rows of tiny twigs poking through dead grasses on both sides of our creek. Their fragile state made me wonder how they would ever survive and grow into a forest. It was going to be a lot of work to help the plants flourish. The kids and I waved goodbye to the workers after they loaded their equipment onto a flatbed trailer and disappeared in a swirl of gravel dust.

Once the CRP project was planted, I turned my attention to our vegetable garden. If the ground was thawed enough to plant trees and shrubs, it was time to dig our plot. I chose a level piece of land that received full sunlight all day long and was adjacent to the ugly block building by the road. A shallow cement trough bordered the north side and was perfect for a compost pile. Alex and I staked out a thirty-foot square with posts and string.

The kids and I tugged on boots and sweatshirts one Sunday morning, then gathered digging implements. I trundled the wheelbarrow, filled with a mix of plastic and metal rakes and shovels, to the spot. But even though the frost was gone, the kids' plastic tools bounced uselessly off the matted grass. I couldn't trust them the dangerous adult tools, so I sent them off to play with a new batch of kittens. Removing the dense sod was labor intensive. After thirty minutes of vigorous effort, I netted a two-foot square cleared spot. A collarless Ellie suddenly materialized and rolled in the rich black dirt.

Grumbling and wondering how she had managed to slip from her tether again, I returned her to the tie out next to Jake. Then I asked Alex, Amie, and Hannah to work the exposed soil while I dug more. That phase of the project proved my theory that the entertainment value of work for children was inversely related to the difficulty of the task. They quickly abandoned their shovels and rakes to play hide-and-go-seek. I envied them.

At my rate of excavation, the garden would be ready for planting the following spring. Disgusted, I threw my shovel on the ground, gathered the children and returned to the house for a warm shower to soothe my aching arms and shoulders. Once I had most of the dirt scrubbed from beneath my fingernails, I fixed a quick lunch. As we sat at the kitchen table eating bowls of chicken noodle soup and grilled cheese sandwiches, that small patch of dark earth mocked me through the kitchen window.

Luckily a neighbor took pity on us. He noticed our project from his rusty pick-up truck and returned on a tractor attached to a chisel plow. It took him fifteen minutes to dig the rest of the plot. Alex and I watched in awe. The only manual work remaining was to smooth over the soil with rakes and toss the clumps of sod into the ditch. I raced into the house and grabbed a handful of freshly baked cookies that Clyde had not yet reached to give our neighbor as a thank-you.

Terry's husband, Ken, became our garden consultant. He told us onions and potatoes could go in early, but all other plants had to wait until the danger of frost was gone. To prevent weeds from getting too much of a head start before the end of May, I covered the plot with a big brown tarp. One day I took the kids to a local greenhouse. The intoxicating perfume of flowers and green plants surrounded us as we wandered inside the steamy glass enclosures. Alex pulled the girls in a bright red wooden wagon, and we stopped often to admire vivid petunias, pansies, and geraniums. We purchased a bag of tiny white onions and a bag of russet potato starters.

A week-long pounding rain transformed our nicely prepared plot into a muddy pit despite the tarp. It took days of spring sunshine before it dried enough to work. At least the forest saplings were getting a great start. One sunny afternoon after preschool, the kids and I approached the garden with the onions and potatoes. Feeling a little foolish, I realized that I had no idea what I was doing and read the directions. What kind of country girl was I? After using the hoe to form a furrow in the ground, I showed the girls how to position the little onions with their green sprouts pointing to the sky and pat earth around them. Alex marked the rows with small wooden stakes. We did the same for the potatoes.

My back muscles protested loudly as I stood up to survey our new garden. There was still plenty of room for tomatoes, peppers, and corn. The children had worked surprisingly well together with a minimum of whining. Ellie and Jake both sported new collars that they were not able to slip out of, so our labor would not be destroyed by them churning up the black dirt.

As May approached the end of her reign on the calendar, we began watching the weather. Once the long-term forecast was free from frost warnings, we returned to the greenhouse and chose several flats of vegetable seedlings, some herbs, and several seed packages. I placed our purchases under one of the silver maples and watered them gently.

The following morning dawned warm and sunny. After breakfast, we pulled on boots, shorts and t-shirts. Then I gathered all the plastic and metal tools into the wheelbarrow again and trundled it over to the flats. But as the kids and I approached them, my heart sank. The delicate plants had been nibbled down to naked stalks. After another expensive trip to the greenhouse, we stored the valuable vegetables on our dining room table and researched garden protection programs. Poisons were not a feasible option; we had too many children, dogs, and kittens that roamed our farm. There was no money in any budget for a perimeter fence. But using small barricades to give the establishing plants some shelter made sense. I rooted around the house for empty milk cartons, frozen orange juice cylinders, and tin cans to repurpose. Using scissors and a can opener, I cut openings in each container to allow sunlight and rain in but keep gnawing teeth out.

The kids and I spent several afternoons placing tomatoes and peppers inside their protectors set in the black dirt. The result was raggedy looking but functional. Alex, Amie and Hannah worked together without fighting, and we finished the remaining garden area by seeding equal rows of sweet corn and green beans. Amie and Hannah discovered tiny green shoots of potatoes and onions poking through the soil in the area we had first planted. The girls were so excited I gently herded them away before the tender plants were trampled.

I turned my attention back to the CRP land. Our contract stipulated the application of an approved herbicide for noxious weed control several times a year. It would give the young saplings a chance to establish their root systems. I diligently followed the package recommendations for the specified product, diluting it with water while wearing a protective mask and gloves. My used four-wheeler (a utilitarian vehicle purchased with the health food store income) was outfitted with a small sprayer unit. I drove it up and down the rows to apply the mixture. It worked great until some of the herbicide landed on some baby red oaks. I felt like a murderer as they withered and died.

After that heart-breaking experience, clearing weeds by hand seemed safer. I spent countless valuable nap time hours yanking tough grass from around the infant river birches, red twig dogwoods, and oaks. By the time the baby monitor summoned me back to the house, I was covered in sweat and insect bites. Sometimes I was able to cajole the kids into helping for a few minutes, but then they invariably wandered off to splash in the creek. Alex, Amie and Hannah were smarter than I; the cold water soothed my itching arms and legs when I joined them.

Tending our garden was not the quaint experience I had known as a child. I remembered my grandmother's stories as we worked side by side, the whispering breeze, and the smells and textures of wax beans and Brussel sprouts. It was not the same fairy tale with our three. The hot sun beat down on my back one afternoon as I pulled ragweed from the corn. I did not see Amie whack Alex with the hoe but cringed when I heard hard plastic meet flesh. After firmly reprimanding her and sending her crying back to the house, a huge bumble bee left our yard of dandelions and buzzed by Hannah. She screamed and raced to the porch. I tossed my rake aside after looking at Alex's back. The ugly red welt needed attention.

I held a frozen bag of peas in place over his wound and slid him a package of fruit snacks to alleviate the pain. He immediately waved it under Amie's nose. Both girls begged for their own treats. Even though I knew it was the wrong thing to do, I emptied the box and gave them each a pack as well. I was just too exhausted to argue with them. At naptime, I fell asleep before they did.

Laboring in the rich black loam became therapeutic and gratifying once I stopped asking the kids for help. Gardening was a welcome change to the overwhelming pasture work. As I bounced back and forth between the two projects that summer, I sometimes wished the amazing weed growth factor on our farm could be extracted, purified, and synthesized. Then we could feed it to our trees and shrubs so they could overshadow the thistles.

When our young tomatoes and peppers reached a decent height, I freed them from their barricades and crossed my fingers. I wasn't sure where the money would come from if we lost another crop. Just as I released the last little Roma plant from its milk carton, a group of Sandhill cranes swooped overhead. I marveled at the rhythmic sound of their wingbeats and hoped they were content eating the new corn and bean plants sprouting in the neighbor's field. Wildlife was plentiful in our neighborhood; I just had to figure out how to cohabitate peacefully with it.

Chicken Strips

Chapter 14

ENCLOSING OUR GRAND FRONT PORCH was the final project to be crossed off on the "Potential Deadly Hazards" list. I had been setting a fund from extra sales at the health food store aside all winter for it. A sturdy rail around its perimeter would allow us to enjoy the stunning views without launching someone into a bone-breaking fall.

Before our move to the farm, flimsy boards nailed haphazardly to posts had been a temporary fix. They were ugly and disintegrating quickly. Another eyesore was an old screened-in portion; its nylon mesh had been shredded by kittens that used it for climbing practice. I believed the task of assembling spindles and rails was achievable without professional intervention. My poor judgement was probably the result of inhaling too many manure fumes when my neighbor spread it as fertilizer in his fields across the road.

Demolishing the old segments of wood-framed screens was much more enjoyable than tearing up the old carpet runner. Less injury-producing as well. The boards were simply screwed into the ceiling and floor and surrendered quickly to my power drill/driver. The frames were in decent shape after we removed the tattered screening, so Alex and I stacked them in the barn workshop just in case we needed them for a different use in the future. Encouraged by the ease of destruction, we moved on to the designing phase. We measured and recorded distances, heights, and widths five times. The frozen bag of peas was only required once, when Amie's fingers got snapped by the measuring tape returning to its home.

There were multiple choices of posts and rails at the big box hardware store. Medium spindles with larger support posts seemed the best option. They were sturdy enough to match the energy of our children and dogs but could be spaced at appropriate intervals to prevent the kids from sticking their heads through. I wasn't sure about the dogs, but hoped Jake, Ellie, and Clyde were smart enough to avoid that scenario. After loading a wobbly cart with supplies (I always grabbed one with wheels that refused to steer straight), I dragged it to the cash register. The kids trailed behind it as a store employee discreetly followed our little parade, replacing merchandise I dislodged along the away. Luckily everything fit into the blue van, including the children.

We entered the building phase. Randy spent several weekends helping. First, additional posts needed to be placed along the perimeter. That required sawing holes through the plywood floor so we could anchor them onto support beams. Multiple shims were required to straighten the posts because nothing about our house was truly horizontal. As soon as the tiny bubbles on Randy's level centered, we bolted the posts in place before they changed their mind. That phase required an entire Saturday and Sunday. I splurged on carry-out pizza from the local bar, and we ate on the sagging steps while the tom cats circled hopefully. They couldn't get past the drooling canines stationed around us who snatched crusts from the air when we tossed them. I was unsure how much Amie or Hannah actually ingested; they had more fun feeding Jake, Ellie, and Clyde.

Assembling the actual rails was more complicated than the posts. The spindles had to be cut to the correct height, fit inside the rails at the right intervals, and then secured. Small thin boards fit into the top and bottom parts between the spindles. A few incorrectly cut boards and not enough screws sent the kids and I on emergency trips to town while Randy continued working. But it was a farm project: destined to never proceed according to plan, stay within budget, or be completed anywhere close to estimated time frames.

There were many choice words muttered as I braced each finished section in place while Randy fastened it to the posts. It was hard work. I envied the kids spraying each other with squirt guns. Even the dogs were having more fun panting in the shade. As soon as Randy and I secured the last section, Hannah tried to get her head between the spindles. She failed. At least all three dogs were able to fit their heads through without getting stuck. The handrail sections for the broad steps were the last and most difficult pieces to build. After a lot of grunting, a little sanding, and a few strong whacks with the hammer, the right side finally fit. But the left side was another story. We looked at its intended span and decided to postpone that last section indefinitely. We had one rail that could be used to get up the steps. The other side was not critical.

Providing protection from the elements was the final step for the porch rail project. I didn't need any help with that. After lugging a gallon of primer up from the basement one day, I gathered brushes that had not been petrified (clean up after painting was not my strong suit) and distracted the kids by showing them gravel stones with tiny veins of shimmering gold. As the children panned for precious metals, I whitewashed in the hot sun. Brushing inside all the nooks and crannies of the rails and spindles took a while. The final product was worth it though; bright white rails marched along the entire expanse of our porch and added much curb appeal to our Victorian farmhouse. Sadly, the fool's gold was worthless.

Our odd assortment of rickety aluminum lawn chairs spread out on the porch floor were unsightly and uncomfortable. We needed something better to enjoy the view. I wanted a porch swing. Alex, Amie, and Hannah agreed. After test driving a few models at the big box hardware store, we dragged a solid cedar A-frame design home.

The following weekend we laid out all the pieces, parts, and instructions on the porch floor. I solemnly pledged to follow directions carefully so my brother wouldn't have to fix anything later. Amie and Hannah sorted screws, bolts, and nuts. Alex and I began assembly. It was not as complicated as the rails had been. At the ripe age of 6, my son had become adept with the power screwdriver. I couldn't wait to teach my daughters how to use it when they were older and less likely to poke an eye out with it. I wanted all my children to learn the life skills I'd fought so hard to acquire.

Even though we carefully followed each step on the wrinkled papers, we still ended up with spare fasteners. But the swing seemed structurally sound, and my brother Randy wholeheartedly approved of our effort (I think he was relieved he didn't have to reassemble it.) That swing became another treasured part of our farm, just like our creek and Barn Town. It gently swayed through countless story times. It was my throne as I watched the kids gather fireflies in jars on warm summer evenings. The breathtaking panorama visible from our front porch swing was a wonderful reminder of why we had moved to the country. It encouraged me to slow down, let the weeds grow a little taller, and forget about other lists for a while.

Front Porch Peach Cobbler

2 c. fresh peaches
3/4 c. sugar
2 eggs
1 c. flour

1 t. baking powder
3/4 c. milk
6 T. butter
1/2 t. mace or nutmeg

Toss thinly sliced peaches with 1/4 c. sugar and mace. Set aside. Put butter in 13x9 pan and put in oven set at 350° until melted. Mix rest of sugar, eggs, flour, milk and baking powder. Pour this over melted butter in pan, spoon peaches on top. Bake 30 minutes or until golden.

Chapter 15

SHRILL BEEPING SLICED INTO MY DREAM of cantering through the countryside astride a long-legged steed of my own. I glared at the alarm clock and smacked the stop button a little harder than necessary. It had been the most pleasurable dream I had had in a long time. Sighing, I slid out from under the covers, threw on some clothes, and quietly shuffled to the bathroom. I had about thirty minutes before the children jumped out of their beds to embrace the summer morning.

Tying my hair back, I grimaced after catching a glimpse of my reflection in the mirror. My hair spiked at odd angles, and my nose was burned. My free-spirit-career-self would not approve. But it didn't matter how I looked for the task ahead, so I brushed my teeth and threw on some sturdy clothes. After stepping over the creaky third step on my way down to the kitchen, I poured myself a cup of coffee, ignored the stack of dirty dishes in the sink, and grabbed the baby monitor instead. The eastern horizon blazed yellow and red through the window. I drained my mug admiring it.

Jake and Ellie eyed me warily, wondering if another bath was imminent after their romp through the cattle yard the night before. Relieved no leashes were taken down from the hooks, they curled back up on their manure-scented carpet. Clyde slipped through the door behind me as I stepped outside. We walked together toward the machine shed. I patted his forehead before gathering my tools.

With a scythe and hoe over my shoulder, I followed Clyde's waving tail. He trotted along the fence line, pausing to sniff posts and rocks. Dew hung heavily on the tall grass and caught the early morning light, forming tiny rainbow prisms. Intricate spider webs woven between the wire fence line and along the ground enticed me to stop and admire their sparkling symmetry. But I couldn't linger long. I had a job to do and marched down the path, dodging the ankle-twisting ant mounds.

At the first row of river birches, I stopped to catch my breath. The little saplings were barely visible between the tall grasses and huge thistles. I dropped my weed cutter to the ground and shrugged my heavy sweatshirt off. After using it to wipe sweat from my face, I tied it loosely around my waist. Battle time.

I'd been spraying around the young plants as outlined by the forestry protocol. But the thistles required weapons beyond the recommended herbicide; it hadn't fazed them. During the next several weeks, my plan was to get up early every morning and reclaim our CRP plot. I donned my thick gloves, picked up the scythe, and addressed my first victim. The plant was taller than me and sprouted eight prickly arms. Each one bore multiple purple blossoms that would later yield thousands of seeds. I took a deep breath and swung the chopper in a short arc. It shaved off two limbs.

"That was not so bad." I said aloud. Hacking away at the rest of the plant, I aimed for several branches at a time. But one of the huge arms dug its sharp spikes into my shoulder just before it fell to the earth-- a final blow before succumbing to fate. I cursed, jumped back, and yanked the offender off with my glove. After plucking the itchy thistle spines from my skin, I stomped on the villainous plant with my boots until it lay flattened on the ground, dead. Justice had been server. Clyde watched from a safe distance.

Ten minutes into the skirmish, I leaned on the chopper handle briefly and surveyed the battlefield. Score: thistles: one (for my injured shoulder) me: seven. Purple flower heads and stalks lay in a crooked path behind me, but my next opponent arrogantly reared before me. Its stalks were at least six inches in diameter. At least, that's what it felt like when my blade connected with them and bounced off. My arms vibrated from the impact. I swore, not so quietly, and aimed for just one branch at a time. My forearms ached, and tiny needles were working their way through my gloves.

After five more minutes, my swings were decidedly less deadly. It was time for a break. I sat on my sweatshirt in the grass, shared a donut with Clyde and washed it down with a few swigs of cool water. Cardinal and robin songs broke the quiet morning. The baby monitor was still quiet. I shut my eyes and leaned back to absorb the warm sun on my face. Maybe a little too warm; I had forgotten sunscreen again. My nose already tingled.

Joints in my knees and ankles cracked loudly when I stood up and stretched. At least two more plants had to go before I returned to the house for a well-earned shower. Whack, whack, whack sounded the cutter. Stop, stop, stop begged my arms. "Three more branches," I muttered under my breath and wondered how farmers of old had done this all day. When the final limb fell, I looked around. Thistle corpses were strewn everywhere, but the numbers of the living still greatly outweighed the fallen. It was going to take a lot longer than originally planned (what a shock), but I had made decent progress in forty minutes. Shouldering my cutter and hoe, I hiked back up the hill with Clyde at my side.

After washing the blade under cold water from the pump near our machine shed, I returned it to its hook in the garden shed. Silence enveloped me as I entered the kitchen. No one was awake yet. I tiptoed into the bathroom, gulped down an antihistamine from the medicine cabinet, and stood under the hot shower until the itching on my hands and arms subsided. Then Hannah cried. Ellie pushed the shower curtain aside with her nose to make sure I had heard. I grinned at her, dried off with a towel so stiff it almost stood up by itself, and began my real day.

For two weeks, I awoke after the sun chased the moon from the sky and dragged my aching body and tools down to the creek. One morning I happily rolled over in bed when thunderstorms rumbled through; Mother Nature knew I needed a break. During that battle period, I was forced to purchase two new cutters after the thistles broke the shaft on one and cracked the blade on the other. But the upside to my war was that my arms and shoulders became nicely chiseled from the work.

I declared a partial victory after two weeks and stopped greeting the day with violence. Instead, I admired the sunrise from our front porch with a cup of coffee and watched our resident red-tailed hawk dive for rodents in the fields. The results of my labor were evident on our post-battle hikes to the pasture; it was not an ocean of purple blossoms anymore. The kids and dogs frolicked amount the seedlings without imminent danger of impalement by thistles.

Spraying excessive herbicides to control thistles was not nearly as satisfying as chopping them down with a scythe. It felt more personal with a hand-to-prickly-octopus-arm battle. And I didn't like adding to the toxic load of our planet any more than necessary. It was going to be a war for years to come, but invasive plants were not going to deny my little trees the chance to grow into a beautiful forest.

Several mornings later, shrieking metal woke me from a deep sleep. It was one of those rare occasions when I hadn't set the alarm clock to accomplish something before the kids woke up. I sighed, threw on sweatpants and stepped out the back door. An aluminum eave outside my bedroom window had released its hold from the roof and dangled against the siding, making the horrible sound. Goodbye sleeping in.

I snapped Jake and Ellie's collars onto their tie outs, then trudged up to the machine shed and retrieved our extension ladder. Clyde followed, and then sprinted after a baby bunny that chose the wrong time to hop across our path. I called Clyde back, even though rabbits were probably the rascals chewing on our radishes. Our golden Labrador meekly followed me as I carried the ladder back to the house.

My heart pounded as I slowly stepped up each rung and then crawled out onto the second story shingles. The roof felt squishy in several places. I took a deep breath, wiggled to the edge, and pounded the metal back into place. Done. As I put excess nails back into my pocket, I admired our beautiful countryside from my high perch. My free-spirit-career-self wanted to zipline down to the ground. The whispering voice envisioned future emergency room visits once the kids realized 1) what a gorgeous view the roof offered and 2) that if they worked together, they could carry the ladder. Tossing my hammer to the ground, I crawled my way back to the ladder, descended, and hid it in a dark corner of the machine shed. It was time to replace our sagging roof before I fell through it.

After stowing my tools in the machine shed, I released Jake and Ellie and let them tow me back to the house. In the kitchen Amie was almost done feeding Hannah yogurt as Clyde cleaned the floor beneath them. Alex quietly read his cereal box. They were such good kids. I grinned. I had intended to start on another project from the DIM list but decided a park and ice cream parlor day sounded better.

The scope of a new roof and windows went far beyond my newly developed finesse with hammer and nail. We needed a professional.

After speaking with several contractors, one person stood out among the stack of written quotes. His name was Todd, and he hit it off with Clyde immediately. Trusting our golden dog's judgment in character was one of our better decisions since moving to the farm. Todd recommended traditional shingles over metal because of the complicated angles and multiple levels of our roof line. I chose a multicolor one which would enhance the faded blue siding.

Windows required custom manufacturing to fit the long and narrow sills of our old house. No inexpensive standard models for us. So, we traveled again to the hardware store (I should have bought stock in the company). Alex and Amie played traveling salesman with the door displays as I looked at different window models with Hannah on my hip. The big kids got a little too excited and slammed a few doors. Then salesperson I was working with sternly told them to be more careful. Tears welled up in their eyes as I firmly grabbed one hand from each, grateful all fingers were still intact, and ordered oak windows with exterior metal frames.

Work began a month later, after the materials were delivered. Scaffolding and ladders circled the house, allowing access to each side. The first phase was removal of the old windows. After a few minor repairs to sills, our new windows were gently lifted into place and secured. Then Todd and his helper began on the roof. I often found Alex shyly watching the carpenters as they tore off old asphalt shingles and threw them into a wagon hitched to a bright green tractor. The last roof layer was made up of ancient shaker shingles that were so rotted they disintegrated when they hit the ground.

Thankfully all the supports were in good shape and didn't need replacing. The next step was to nail down plywood sheeting and cover it with tar paper. Todd and his co-worker gracefully navigated the steep surfaces as they worked. I admired their strength when they hoisted heavy bundles of shingles on their shoulders and carried them up the scaffolding. I could barely lift one package. They labored from sunrise to sunset, making the most of long summer days. When they ate their lunch beneath a shady maple tree, Alex or Amie delivered a plate of freshly baked cookies to them.

We held our first (and last) garage sale during our roof construction. Excited with the possibility of making money, the kids lined up their old toys on tables set up in the barn and wrote prices on stickers borrowed from our store. Alex rediscovered the joy of his plastic race tracks and metal cars and set them up in the living room so I would have something to stumble over later. Amie and Hannah quietly smuggled several stuffed animals back into the house. I pretended not to notice.

We placed signs by the highway early one morning and eagerly waited for cars to arrive. Alex posted himself on the front porch, alerting the girls and I via the baby monitor to potential customers traveling down the road. Amie and Hannah played in the barn and shooed tom cats away from tables of clothes before they managed to curl up on them. The first wave of shoppers arrived, and we watched them optimistically as they rifled through our wares. They asked a lot of questions about our family and eyed me up and down; I was thankful Clyde never left my side as they browsed.

As the day wore on, the kids became dispirited. A grand total of twenty dollars was in our shoe box. The wind picked up and dark clouds gathered on the western skyline; I took the clothes off the line and fed the kids lunch. Just as I was putting the milk back in the refrigerator, one of our neighbors pulled into our lane. I met him at the back door. "You'd better keep the kids inside – big storm coming – winds over seventy miles an hour reported in Iowa." He hopped back into his truck, threw it into reverse, and raced up the road to warn the other neighbors. I herded the kids to the barn to close things up. Todd's crew covered the exposed plywood with a blue tarp and left for their own homes.

From the barn hill, we saw a straight line of black clouds heading toward us. Just as we closed the heavy sliding doors, our babysitter pulled into our lane with her two children. I ushered everyone inside the house; a wind gust slammed the door behind us. As tree limbs danced madly outside the living room window, I realized it was probably time to take shelter in the basement.

Rain pelted the thick stone walls and small basement windows as the storm howled. My children hovered next to me. I was afraid too. And then, as quickly as it had arrived, the squall moved on. I cautiously walked up to the kitchen and peeked through the door to make sure it was safe. Clyde licked Amie's face happily after he jumped out of the cast iron tub. He had probably chosen the safest place of all. After our impromptu guests left, the kids and I surveyed the farm. The maples had shed several big branches, but that was the only damage we saw.

The signs announcing our garage sale had blown away. From our front porch we spotted uprooted trees in the pasture across from us. Then our neighbor drove up again, his expression sober. "Did you see the other side of your barn?" he asked. I shook my head. We all ran up to the main doors. Alex and Amie arrived first; juggling Hannah on my hip slowed me. When I tugged open the sliders, air rushed past us. The display tables had been overturned and our carefully arranged items were strewn across the wooden floor. The wood panel on the southern side had been ripped away as well as part of the eastern wall.

Alex, Amie, and Hannah gathered toys and clothes and placed them back into boxes. I erected an impromptu barrier with the orange snow fence in front of the gaping holes. After cleaning what we could, we trudged back to the house. I called Todd and explained what had happened. He gave me contact information for a crew that would have the right equipment to work on the huge structure. The storm had been particularly vicious in his neighborhood, and they were busy helping neighbors who had lost roofs and sheds.

After several days of piecing together insurance information, repair estimates, and cleaning up the mess, the company we chose delivered their lift and supplies to the farm. They replaced the shattered barn boards, asbestos panels, and windows in a week. Todd returned to complete the final touches on our project after his storm clean-up was done. On their final day, before he readied the tractor to drive the backroads home, the kids and I delivered an applesauce-filled German pancake for lunch. Feeding him and his crew was the least we could do to thank them for our beautiful new roof and windows. Todd said goodbye as he gently tugged Alex's hat down over his eyes and patted Clyde. He had become a wonderful friend. We invited him to visit anytime.

Rita's German Pancake

½ c. milk
2 T. butter
chopped nuts

½ c. flour
3 eggs
fresh berries

Preheat oven to 400°. Melt 1 T. butter in pie plate while oven is preheating. In a bowl, melt the rest of the butter and whisk in other ingredients along with a pinch of salt and vanilla. Pour into pie plate and bake 10-15 minutes until puffed and golden. Sprinkle with powdered sugar.

Chapter 16

IN THE SUBURBS, SOUNDS OF POUNDING hammers and buzzing saws filled the air as subdivisions of cookie cutter homes blossomed over the landscape. Families looking to escape the city had their choice of three or four floor plans and several exterior colors to make construction fast and easy. Fancy subdivision names were declared at grand entrances. I figured someone found an empty liquor bottle in the field that became Tanqueray Meadows, a very exclusive development sprouting mansions like mushrooms. At least it was original.

Housing was different in the country. Most of the land was still farmed; urban sprawl had not reached our little corner of the Midwest. Rural properties were unique in appearance and much older than their suburban counterparts. They also had rich histories. We unearthed a few intriguing relics while working around our buildings. A corroded pressing iron, wooden downhill skis, and an ancient sled with rusty metal runners whispered hints of lives before us. We really didn't know anything about families who had cooked their dinners in our kitchen or milked their cows in the barn. Until one autumn day.

Clyde needed professional medical attention after tangling with a nasty groundhog. He had some deep cuts that went beyond my ability with gauze pads and tape. We loaded him into the van and drove to our local veterinarian. The assistant perked up when she entered our address on her computer. She smiled and told us she had grown up on our farm. While the doctor tended to Clyde, she entertained the kids and I with its history.

German immigrants purchased the original one-hundred eighty-acre parcel in the late 1800's. The original house, complete with a summer kitchen for canning, had boasted a cistern and an outhouse but only two bedrooms. Needing more space to accommodate seven children, the family purchased a nearby home which had been vacant for some time. Legend had it that its elderly owners had been murdered there. No one had dared set foot over its lonely threshold. Undeterred by its haunted reputation, the father and his sons employed a team of mules and horses to move the structure from its foundation and attach it to their house.

All work was done manually or via horsepower in those early times. In addition to draft horses and cows, the family raised pigs and chickens. The farm received electricity in 1923. That modernized the milking process and enabled them to increase their dairy herd. An indoor bathroom with hot and cold running water was added. The farm was handed down to the next family for three generations.

Over the years, land around the house was dedicated to a large fruit orchard, walnut grove, and multiple vegetable gardens. Our storyteller reminisced of herding and milking cows before heading off to school. After classes, she helped her mother preserve their produce. I glanced at Alex, Amie, and Hannah's faces to make sure they were listening. Despite the long and sometimes difficult days, our new friend fondly remembered the farm as a wonderful place to grow up. Sadly, the apple and peach trees, along with the gardens, had been tilled under for more grain crops by the family who was two owners before us. The walnut trees were harvested and sold for lumber.

Our farm's history was fascinating, even though part of it had been a scene to a grisly crime. But of the thousands of worries that circled my head at night, unhappy spirits were not among them. Occasionally Alex or Amie summoned me to their rooms after bad dreams, convinced there was a monster in their closet. But the noises they heard were more likely mice searching for food the kids had smuggled upstairs. Jake, Ellie, and Clyde slept peacefully, unconcerned with ethereal presences. I trusted their instincts.

We thanked the veterinarian after Clyde came out of the exam room, stitched together and happy to see us. As we paid the bill, the assistant wished us luck. Then our big golden dog dragged me out the door; he was ready to go home. I was too. Enchanted by the stories of our farm's past, an idea started to form in the back of my mind. Instead of being known as "the farm that belonged to so-and-so who bought it from you-know-who who sold it to that couple," I wanted to brand the farm as our own. Best of all, my plan wouldn't cost much money.

Keeping rural buildings protected from the elements involved a lot of paint. And it had to be reapplied frequently, because even the strongest enamel was no match for the Midwest's crazy temperature fluctuations, relentless rains, strong sun, and abrasive snows. Between fixing and patching minor items, a totally separate to-do list had arisen, devoted only to tasks involving primer, brushes, and paint.

Painting was simple, satisfying, and a pleasant alternative to chopping thistles and pulling weeds. Amie, Alex, and Hannah also enjoyed wielding brushes, especially after they saw the result of adding a little color to their bedrooms. They had helped a bit when I whitewashed the porch rails and spindles, but the tight spaces proved too tedious. Kids did better with bigger areas. So, when I decided my first building would be the milk shed, three little helpers immediately gathered as I pried open the lid from a gallon of paint. I handed them each a brush. Hannah worked beside me. Alex and Amie started at the other end. Robins chirped as they carried twigs and grasses to their nest under the eaves. Swishing brushes was the only other sound for a few minutes. Then Amie accidentally splattered paint on Alex's arm. He threw his brush at her. She ducked, and the fully paint-loaded projectile hit Hannah on the head instead.

Sighing, I refastened the lid to prevent kittens from falling in and marched my crying children into the house. It took a while to scrub all the whitewash from faces, arms, and hair. After that, they raced off to play in Barn Town while I finished the first wall. It took several weeks to complete the milk shed; I still had to chop thistles, weed the garden, and feed the kids. But once done, the white boards were a big improvement over greying, peeling wood. I had space for my idea.

We couldn't afford any real farm animals yet, but imaginary ones were free. By the time the kids awoke from nap time one afternoon, a black and white rooster crowed on the door of the milk shed. Next week, silhouettes of three Holstein calves cavorted on the doors of our garden shed. After a month, a curious goat peeked out of a boarded-up window on the lower level of the barn, while a mare and her foal trotted on one of the machine shed's huge doors. Neighbors began to comment on how much the murals improved our farm's appearance. Farmers checking their corn fields four miles to the north often drove the long way around to see my latest project.

As we spent more time playing in Barn Town, I realized rain was seeping through the roof's disintegrating shingles and leaving puddles on the floors. Preserving that grand structure was worth investing in. We needed a metal roof that would last, so we hired the same company who had fixed the storm damage the year before. They delivered materials two weeks later. Alex and I watched the workers as they used a mechanical lift to install steel panels over the timbers. My mind went into overdrive with new mural possibilities if I could access upper levels. After sketching several ideas, I settled on a simple design that would be visible as soon as visitors crested our hill (and hoped the workers would let me borrow their equipment).

The next day I gathered enough courage to ask the foreman if I could use their lift for a project. He did not deny my request right away, so I kept my fingers crossed while I mowed the yard and took the kids for a hike. As the crew ended another day of construction and put away their tools, the foreman found me in the vegetable garden weeding pepper plants. He asked if I still wanted to use the lift. I eagerly nodded and followed him to the other side of the barn where he gave me a short course in its operation. The kids all begged for rides. Imagining three little bodies dangling from that cage gave me the shivers. I made a quick phone call to Becky so I could create my masterpiece without interruptions.

It took multiple practice runs up and down before I felt comfortable with the controls. It wasn't a pretty sight; I held on tight as the bucket lurched, bucked, and sounded alarms. The foreman would have immediately rescinded my privileges had he witnessed my efforts. Alex offered to help but I'd observed his questionable driving skills in Barn Town. I felt safer on my own.

I decided to practice working at heights by painting the barn's window frames first. Several had raw wood showing. There were three in all, two on the second story and one on the third. Becky and the kids perched on the cement cattle feeder to watch. Painting the highest window was terrifying, especially when I accidentally looked down. I whitewashed with one hand and white-knuckled the bucket rails with the other. Wasps buzzed angrily at my invasion of their space. I dodged them, slapped paint on that frame as quickly as I could, then descended to the second story windows. My stomach was a lot less queasy there and the wasps returned to their gigantic nest in the roof peak. I made a mental note to deal with them later.

Once the window frames were done, I lowered the lift to the ground. Except for a few splatters on the top window, the frames looked pretty good. So, I retrieved my plan from the kitchen counter and re-ascended with Amie's favorite purple sidewalk chalk. Copying the lines from my drawing exactly, I worked the lift around until the sketch was done. Then I guided the bucket smoothly down for a preview. Beating a pretend drum roll in my mind, I eagerly looked up at my outline. And my heart plummeted. The beast I had drawn looked more like a prehistoric rat than the elegant running horse I had envisioned. Where had I gone wrong? I looked from my paper to the building and back. Then it hit me: my graph paper was gridded in squares, but the asbestos shingles on the barn were rectangles! Rolling my eyes, I hopped back up into the lift and resorted to free handing like usual. The new drawing was better. I decided to sleep on it before permanently tattooing the barn.

The next morning, the sun's rays shone on my outline as if Mother Nature even approved of the design. After the workers finished for the day, I hopped in the lift and started to fill my outline with black paint. Each brush stroke added more life to the silhouette as I moved the bucket back and forth. Just before I lowered the lift for the final time, I took it up to the peak and sprayed the wasp nest. There was no guilt; they'd stung me several times. Back on the ground, I parked the machine, gathered my materials, opened the bucket gate, and plunged my left foot into a fresh cow pie. I laughed at the humbling reminder of country life. As the kids, Becky, and I admired our new farm landmark, my free-spirit-career-self whispered "Bravo."

Instead of being known as the farm that belonged to the "family-who-moved-from-the-suburbs-and-paid-too-much-money," our property became known as "Running Horse Farm" in honor of my latest work.

While overhearing a farmer discuss my paintings with the teller at our local bank one day, I grinned. We hadn't met yet, but we both wore the same type of rubber boots that smelled faintly of manure. Our family was slowly becoming part of the community, and we were adding our own style to the farm's history. I was not sure if the land, buildings, and house were becoming an extension of my personality, or if they were taking over mine. I was ok with either.

Chapter 17

ONE FACTOR WE HADN'T GIVEN MUCH THOUGHT to since our move to the country was how distant we were from accessible healthcare. It was a convenience we had taken for granted while living on the urban grid. Luckily our rural first aid experiences were limited to scraped knees and bumps that could be fixed by colorful band aids and kisses. Nothing life-threatening. Until one summer day.

Alex, Amie, and Hannah were running through a sprinkler set up in the front yard under the hot July sun. Barefoot and laughing, they shrieked when the icy water pelted their skin. I smiled as I watched from the porch steps. Sweat trickled down my back as I scanned the tattered pages of our lawn mower manual for instructions on changing the belt again. It was the third one I'd shredded in a month. A throaty engine growl encouraged me to look up and wave to our neighbor as he drove by on his tractor. I gave up on the mower, grabbed a squirt gun and surprised the kids as they sailed the little sailboat my father was storing at our farm on an imaginary ocean of long green grass.

We docked our vessel, and all ran through the cold spray one more time. Suddenly our neighbor pulled into our lane and motioned me toward him. I trotted over and stood next to a tractor tire as tall as I was, embarrassed by my bikini top and cutoff jeans. He did not notice; his usual ruddy cheeks were very pale. He stammered that he'd been stung by some bees and asked if we could take him to a doctor. I tried to convince him to leave his tractor where it stood and get into our vehicle. But he was adamant that we pick him up at his house after he changed clothes. I let him drive off after realizing we were wasting precious seconds arguing.

I shut off the sprinkler and herded the kids into the van, tossing random shoes in after them. Hannah's diaper smelled relatively clean when I hoisted her into the car seat. I asked Alex to help Amie buckle her safety belt. I raced into the house to grab my keys, backpack, and a shirt, snagging two towels off the front porch rail for good measure.

An idea hit me as we backed down the lane. I slammed the van back into drive, parked, and retrieved a bottle of antihistamine from our medicine cabinet. As I put the van into reverse, I handed the emergency stash of goldfish crackers under my seat to Alex. Instructing him to give some to the girls, I hit the accelerator. And realized I was still barefoot too. But I didn't want to waste time looking for shoes for myself. After skidding around the corner onto the neighbor's lane, I pulled up to their house, ran up their front steps and knocked on the door. No response. I pounded harder. Finally, my neighbor appeared in the doorway; clean clothes had not improved his appearance. I helped him into the passenger seat of the van and handed him the Benadryl.

We flew up gravel roads toward the closest hospital I knew of, just over the Wisconsin border, spewing rocks and sand in our wake. Our neighbor slurred that he was seeing double, so I told him to drink some of the medicine. I glanced over and grabbed it from him before he drained it. The kids were silent. Thankfully we did not meet any slow-moving farm machinery while we bounced up and down the steep hills. Once we reached the highway, I pushed the speedometer past seventy and hoped the police were busy elsewhere.

The ten minutes required to drive twelve miles felt like two hours. I talked about the weather and asked silly questions about cows to keep our neighbor awake. Dodging traffic and keeping our speed just below what was legal once we reached town, I finally screeched to a halt in front of the emergency entrance. As quickly as I could, I released everyone from their seats and led our neighbor to the receptionist, hoping the kids would follow. My jumbled story alarmed her, and she swiftly took him back to an examination room after staring wide-eyed at our raggedy group. Amie held Hannah's little hand tightly and Alex carried a giant yellow squirt gun that he had apparently smuggled along as protection from people in white coats.

I was not sure about rules for footwear in a hospital. Our lack of them probably did not meet sanitation guidelines. After gently disarming Alex, I told the children to stay in the waiting room while I parked the van and retrieved shoes for everyone. When I returned, they were all sitting peacefully in chairs watching a cartoon show courtesy of a grandmotherly woman sitting in one of the plastic chairs. I gave Hannah her blanket, got shoes on everyone, and settled in a seat myself. My adrenaline rush was fading.

"We drove like our wild realtor lady, huh, buddy?" I asked Alex. He cautiously smiled, still convinced a vaccination might be imminent. Just then, a nurse pushed through the grey metal swinging doors and asked me how much antihistamine our neighbor had ingested. I gave her what was left of the bottle. Luckily that was part of their standard protocol along with steroids and epinephrine. She reported that he was a little groggy, but stable. His wife was on her way to the hospital, and he had requested to see the kids.

Alex, Amie, Hannah, and I followed the nurse's blue scrubs down the hall. The kids each grasped some part of my body as we walked into our neighbor's room. Beeping and blinking machines surrounded his bed. Some of the color had returned to his cheeks and he smiled when we walked in. He groggily explained that while cultivating, the plow blades had dug up a hive from the ground. The doctor estimated that over 200 bees had stung his arms, legs, and chest. Amie walked over to him and shyly took his offered hand. Alex hovered near my leg until he was finally coaxed to shake the other hand solemnly. Hannah refused to leave her perch on my hip but did peek out from under her blanket several times.

Our neighbor's wife arrived, hugged us all, and thanked us for our help. We escaped the sterile room as quickly as possible after saying goodbye. I thanked the elderly woman before we paraded out of the hospital and smiled as everyone crawled back into the van. My heart had finally slowed its pounding, and the kids were back to their usual bickering. I realized that we had missed lunch and decided to splurge.

As we wound our way from the fast-food order speaker to the pick-up window, I sent a silent thank you skyward. My children had behaved incredibly well during the emergency, and I was proud. None of them had wandered off into the labyrinth of hospital hallways, our neighbor was going to be fine, and I had escaped a speeding ticket. It was rare that we indulged in the salty goodness of French fries and chicken nuggets, but we deserved a treat.

The heavy scent of greasy fried food filled the van as I handed a kid's meal to each child and started sipping my strawberry shake. I drove us back to the farm well under the speed limit, thinking how fortunate we were to have been home when our neighbor needed help. It could have happened on one of my days at the health food store, when the kids were at the babysitter's house. Making a mental note to sign up for CPR and first aid training, I turned onto our gravel road a bit too sharply. Amie spilled ketchup on her seat, Hannah dropped her remaining nuggets on the floor and Alex's toy flew out of his hand and hit my head-- things I usually became upset about. The bees had reminded me how precious life was. Clyde greeted us as soon as we pulled into the lane, and Jake and Ellie barked from the dining room windows. I herded my crew of tired kids into the house and gathered them close on the couch to watch a movie. Our dogs sprawled around us, happy we were home.

I struck out for the third time during a neighborhood softball game a few weeks later. Figuring I would do the least damage in the outfield, I jogged to midfield. Then our neighbor, who had recovered fully, hit a fly ball, and sent me into the cornfield. He leisurely jogged to home base as I carefully poked through the rows until I found the ball. My team was losing, but no one cared. We were all having fun and looking forward to our potluck lunch. The tale of our hospital adventure had spread through the rural grapevine rapidly, and I received quite a bit of ribbing about racing our old van along backroads in a swimsuit with three shoeless children. I didn't mind. The story had a very happy ending.

Chicken Strips

Chapter 18

DESPITE DILIGENT WEEDING THROUGHOUT spring and summer, our vegetables fared poorly. Our harvest of onions and potatoes was dismal; apparently, we had not planted the starters deep enough. The sweet corn was ravaged by raccoons, green beans drowned in heavy rains, and huge worms infested the broccoli. The only plants that had done well were the tomatoes. They had taken over the entire garden.

As I stood surrounded by vines laden with round red produce one August morning, I realized I was going to need help. I offered Alex, Amie and Hannah fifty cents per bucketful of tomatoes taken up to the house. Overloading the plastic buckets was disastrous; tears welled up in Amie's eyes as she stood over the splattered remains of her first load. I kissed her on the forehead and told her there were plenty more. Jake and Ellie, who had managed to slip through their tighter collars, happily gobbled up the pieces before galloping merrily to the creek in search of manure. I sighed and let them go. At the garden, we found our rhythm where Hannah and I gathered, Alex shuttled buckets to the porch with the four-wheeler, and Amie carried them inside the house.

I'd forgotten how delicious homegrown tomatoes were. The ones grown on our rich Midwest soil under the thick humidity and sunshine tasted so much better than grocery store offerings. We feasted on bacon, lettuce, and tomato sandwiches and hearty salads. But after several weeks, the kids refused to consume any more. Hundreds remained on the vines, so we picked all the ripe ones one Saturday and went to town for our first experience at the farmers' market. Our little table sold out quickly, mostly due to the children's cuteness factor. They made enough to purchase their own boxes of fruit snacks.

At the end of August, I registered Alex for half-day kindergarten. He was assigned the morning session. After we purchased school supplies and a backpack for my first-born, all four of us celebrated with sundaes at our favorite ice cream parlor. It was the beginning of a new era. A week later, the girls and I waved from the end of our lane as he slid into the front seat behind our neighbor (the same bee incident farmer) who drove the rumbling yellow bus.

We settled into a new routine (again.) On my days off from the health food store, the girls and I picked tomatoes after Alex boarded the bus. Amie and Hannah carried buckets from the garden to the house. The not-quite-ready tomatoes were set in pans on the porch steps to ripen during the day and brought inside at night. The rest found spots in the house. Every cookie sheet and baking container held tomatoes. Our dining room table was no longer visible beneath all the produce. We were living in a crimson ocean that would turn into mush if I didn't figure out what to do with it. I made a desperate call to Terry for help.

She laughed understandingly; she was facing the same issue and had been canning for weeks. The first step was to boil the tomatoes for a few minutes, plunge them into an ice bath, and slide the skins off. It was a messy, time-consuming job. After draining, the good parts were all cooked together. I spent my free days skinning, cooking, and ladling tomatoes into jars. Chopping and cleaning made my fingers and hands raw. I was in a tomato prison, chained to my stove and cutting board. There was no end in sight; the damn plants continued to produce in an unseasonably warm fall.

The only other plants that flourished that summer were five spindly raspberry plants imported from our suburban garden. They had multiplied exponentially. The ripe red berries were as big as my thumb, sweet and juicy. Our late summer menus featured raspberry pancakes, raspberry coffee cake, chocolate cupcakes with raspberries, and raspberry-topped vanilla ice cream. But we couldn't keep up with them, just like the tomatoes. I again consulted with Terry, who gave me a box of pectin and instructions for raspberry jam.

Homemade raspberry jam boosted the status of our peanut butter and jelly sandwiches to gourmet. It was so much better than store bought varieties. And just when I was ready to surrender to our prolific produce, we awoke to find the ground covered in delicate white frost. I rejoiced and was grateful as I placed the lids on my final canning batches. Everyone on our holiday list that year received a festive jar of stewed tomatoes and red raspberry jam in their gift basket.

Chapter 19

KEEPING UP WITH CURRENT TRENDS had never been important to me. I didn't care about fancy cars or name brands. But I did like things clean and uncluttered. It hadn't been an issue at our small suburban house; modern appliances and easy to care for floors helped me keep everything tidy. Not the same with our farmhouse. Three creek-loving young children and three filth-seeking mongrels raced constantly through our rambling farmhouse, spreading dirt from the back door through the mud porch, kitchen, dining room, and back outside through the screened front door.

My definition of housekeeping evolved. Picking violets with the kids or throwing tennis balls for our mongrels took priority over scrubbing floors. Hannah's pediatrician would have been pleased. The kitchen had become the hub of our home, where I spent a lot of my waking hours making meals, serving meals, cleaning up after meals, and chasing after dogs who snatched unguarded meals. It was where we lived. Even though the appliances were more yellowed than white, they worked. Three of the stove burners lit with coaxing, the oven baked if we used the middle rack, and I managed to stuff what we needed inside the ancient refrigerator.

During our second summer, the inside refrigerator light mysteriously died. After weeks of groping around in the dark and knocking over bottles, I changed the bulb. It did not help. The power supply checked out correctly, so apparently something was wrong in the wiring. It would probably have cost more than the refrigerator was worth to call a technician in. And there was the huge obstacle of finding someone willing to drive miles of dirt roads to even begin a service call.

Living without a refrigerator light wasn't the worst situation. After all, if the wiring was bad, the rest of the working parts could not be long for this world either. So, I let it hum away in its corner, waiting for it to sputter and die. Months flew by. Busy days on the farm and hectic weeks at the health food store left me too exhausted to pursue late night television and its accompanied snacking. It was too much work to forage for edibles inside that dark depths of that appliance anyway.

Eventually, duct tape held the refrigerator door handle together and secured most of the shelves. But it continued to keep things cold. And dark. Occasionally I cleaned out the contents during daylight hours in a frenzied effort to determine a source of obnoxious odors. Sometimes I just dumped everything questionable together into the dog dishes; it had to taste better than the decomposed carcasses they dragged home.

One gloomy autumn day, I sat on the kitchen floor once again surrounded by containers and baggies filled with unknown substances. They smelled so bad that Jake and Ellie did not even try to slink away with them. No amount of scrubbing removed the dried spaghetti sauce under the produce tray or the hamburger juice beneath the cheese unit. I tossed my disgusting proverbial towel on the dirty linoleum and declared the old appliance had to go.

We scheduled a field trip to the huge appliance warehouse after the kids "helped" at our health food store the next Saturday. Shiny models filled several aisles with options. Alex, Amie, and Hannah were mesmerized by one that had a television in the door. Our choices were mind-boggling: glass shelves versus plastic, white versus stainless steel, side by side refrigerator/freezer, freezer on the bottom, and the traditional top freezer. And they all had working interior lights; some even in the freezer sections.

The kids and I stayed within our budget and chose a simple plain white model with easily cleanable shelves and sturdy door handles to withstand constant opening and closing. After our new unit was delivered, the old refrigerator was hauled away to the dump. I bet it would still work if we unearthed it and plugged it in today. Its unmarred replacement proudly stood in its place and easily accommodated everything we loaded onto the pristine non-spaghetti-sauce-stained shelves. Sometimes, late at night, I opened the door just to gaze fondly at its brightly illuminated interior.

Chapter 20

AS I TURNED THE PAGES of a scrapbook for Amie and Hannah one September morning, I realized it had been several years since our move. The only places they recognized were the fire station where we celebrated Alex's third birthday and the Tastee Freeze. They had been too young to remember the trip to Shedd Aquarium and Museum of Science and Industry with their cousins. My free-spirit-career-self urged me to revisit the city; she didn't want my children to grow up fearing crowded urban areas.

Then I discovered Terry and Jody had never wandered downtown Chicago. We had started our quilting group up again after canning season ended and were working on wall hangings. I coaxed them into coming along for our urban adventure. My motives were both altruistic and selfish: a 3 on 3 defense with the children gave me better odds than 1 on 3. The plan received wholehearted approval from my free-spirit-career-self who was basking in a sunny California vineyard sipping Pinot Grigio.

Alex, Amie, and Hannah were seasoned travelers after all the business and farm hunting trips they had endured. They were also good sports about my tendency to get lost. Traveling by car was more intimate with the countryside and made it easier to explore curiosities along the way. Containment inside our own vehicle was good for everyone; trains and airplanes risked exposing fellow travelers to unpredictable temper tantrums and inconsolable crying that I couldn't control. Above all, road trips were a family tradition. My parents had hauled me and my brothers in a station wagon every summer to a Wisconsin fishing lodge for vacation. Sandwiched in the back seat between my brothers, we fought, played games, and pelted our parents with questions for five hours each way. I wasn't going to deprive my children of those same rich experiences.

When we lived in the suburbs, I had taken the kids on a voyage to North Carolina for a family reunion. I thought traveling on my own with three small children would be fun; clearly my reasoning abilities had been damaged by childbirth. We headed south one sunny morning in a van filled with suitcases, coolers, beach balls, and high hopes. An ancient portable television played movies while I untangled maps and navigated highways. It was a challenge, being the solo adult required serious concentration to make sure no one disappeared along the way. At hotels, I loaded the children onto a luggage cart along with their little overnight bags. On the road, we picnicked at interstate rest areas where I could watch all three easily. Miraculously, all four of us arrived at our destination with everyone happy and accounted for, even though the television self-destructed the second day of our journey. Chicago would be a piece of cake.

As we left our rolling fields behind, Jody and Terry voiced concerns about muggings and murders. I grinned and assured them that I knew how to avoid the dangerous areas. It was just a little white lie. Subdivisions and industrial parks quickly replaced barns, silos, and alfalfa fields. Cars and trucks crowded the black highway, and after about an hour the kids excitedly watched planes descend toward the international airport. Four lanes of traffic grew into six, and we merged onto one of the main arteries leading downtown. Jody gripped my map between white knuckles.

We exited off the expressway and weaved our way through busy streets to what I remembered as a good parking garage. Other vehicles gave our dusty van a wide berth. We found the right building, and a little white ticket popped out from the machine when I pushed the button. Maneuvering slowly through the narrow labyrinth, I finally found a spot that would accommodate our large vehicle. While everyone tumbled out of the van, I assembled the stroller, shouldered my backpack of snacks and juice boxes, and cajoled Amie and Hannah into their seats. Terry and Jody held Alex's small hands firmly as we headed to the elevator.

The parking garage reeked of urine and garbage. We all held our noses as the old elevator lurched down and delivered us to the sidewalk. Couriers sped by on bicycles in the streets and suited workers briskly walked between tall office buildings. Panhandlers held cups out to pedestrians. It was a different world from cows gently lowing to their calves and tall grasses whispering in the breeze. The six of us huddled a little closer together and walked toward my first landmark, the old water tower that was the sole survivor of the Chicago fire.

We gawked at high-priced merchandise displayed in shop windows along Michigan Avenue. Carriage drivers skillfully guided their horses through busy streets and parked at strategic spots to hawk for fares. Amie and Hannah climbed out of the stroller to pet several velvety noses. Later that afternoon I coaxed everyone down to Oak Street Beach, where we waded in the frigid Lake Michigan water until our feet became numb. A trip to the city was not complete without a visit to one of its tallest buildings. I had doubts whether my three would stand in the long elevator line at Sears Tower, so we opted to take a free ride to the top of the John Hancock building. The vistas from the bathroom windows were simply stunning.

By dinner time, our necks were sore from craning constantly upward. My feet protested their lack of freedom; I was used to going barefoot.

The children were tired and hungry. We found an old-fashioned diner where the staff sang and danced as they served food. Amie and Hannah were enthralled by the show, while Alex sat near the window to watch emergency vehicles scream by. The cost of a burger, fries and a milk shake (fifteen dollars!) was a shock.

After three little faces were scrubbed clean, our weary band retraced the path to our parking garage, rode the rusted elevator back up, and crawled back into the van. After paying the parking fee, I piloted us away from the urban jungle. All three kids fell asleep before we reached the expressway. Jody and Terry chatted about the highlights of our day and commented that the city really wasn't such a scary place after all. I smiled. Mission accomplished.

Bright streetlamps and neon signs were gradually replaced by dark fields and blue farmyard lights. Sipping coffee from my splurge of the day, a souvenir mug, I changed the radio station from urban alternative music to country. I munched on some homemade granola I'd stashed in my backpack, and kept an eye out for deer and raccoons crossing the roads. Everyone was asleep, which gave me plenty of time to think. The city's energy, excitement, and opportunities made it a wonderful place to visit, but I had no desire to live near such crowded areas anymore. The country was where I belonged, and where my children had room to run.

When we topped the last large hill before exiting the highway, the night view of our valley took my breath away. Before me, the white and amber lights of our small town twinkled gently as if to welcome us home. I turned down our gravel road, dropped Jody and Terry off at their farms, and headed to the farmhouse. A warm yellow light glowed from the kitchen window. Clyde trotted down from his front porch post and followed me as I carried each slumbering child inside and up to their bedrooms. Jake and Ellie sniffed me with interest as I turned off lights and headed upstairs. They probably remembered more of their urban lives than the kids did. Especially Jake, the dumpster dog. After I collapsed into my bed, both dogs jumped up and curled beside me. Crickets sang softly through my open window, and I smiled out at the star-studded sky. We were where we belonged.

Farmhouse Granola

- ¼ c. butter
- ⅓ c. honey
- vanilla
- dried fruit
- ½ c. coconut flakes
- 2 c. instant oats
- raw nuts and seeds ✱
- sea salt

Preheat oven to 325°. Grease 13x9 pan. Melt butter and honey, then add vanilla and salt. Fold in nuts and seeds. Spread in pan and bake until golden. When cool, add dried fruit & store in mason jar.

✱ Cashews, sunflower seeds, and dried tart cherries are my favorite.

Chapter 21

AS A MOTHER IN HER LATE THIRTIES with a to-do list a mile long, it was easy to get stuck in serious work mode. A little levity was necessary to counterbalance the formidable responsibilities of parenting, proprietorship, and land stewardship. Weekly evenings with Jody and Terry lifted my spirits and provided helpful guidance whenever I struggled with parental dilemmas. But I needed a daily dose of happiness in addition to their support. It had to be inexpensive. Maybe a morning yoga practice? Evening meditation? The answer appeared unexpectedly one day, in a bright, whimsical store window display-- and changed my attitude toward underwear forever.

Purchasing undergarments had never been an exciting experience. I'd grown up in plain white underwear that my mother had insisted upon. B.C. (before children), my free-spirit-career-self had occasionally splurged on fancy lingerie for special occasions. But the scratchy lace and uncomfortable scraps of material wedged their way into places I didn't want them. Those items, along with the horrifying maternity underwear I'd worn with each pregnancy, met their demise in a suburban landfill before we moved. When the elastic gave out on my current utilitarian underwear style, I simply tossed packages of uninspired brands into our shopping cart.

Sweet-natured Hannah was going through some of her terrible twos. I dropped Amie and Alex off for a play date and took the screamer with me. We drove to a local mall to find a baby shower gift for a friend (stewed tomatoes just did not seem appropriate). Pushing the stroller quickly to drown out her cries, I stopped for a minute to adjust the belt she strained against. Suddenly she fell silent. I followed her line of vision and found myself also mesmerized by the beautiful bright pink, purple, and blue colors in the display window of a lingerie shop. I aimed the stroller inside the unexpected oasis of toddler calm.

Several women close to my age browsed the fancy bras and perfumes. A group of giggling high school girls dug through bins of thongs. One man sat in a velvet chair watching his wife/girlfriend/lover as she rifled through a rack of black teddies, corsets, and other configurations I couldn't even name. She coyly asked his opinion of several; his face traveled through the entire red color spectrum while he stuttered an answer. I stifled a laugh and pushed Hannah past them to a sale table displaying panties of every rainbow shade imaginable.

Hannah began to squirm, but I rocked the stroller while I chose some brightly colored briefs and dashed to the check-out counter with my choices. The sales lady wrapped my purchases in fluffy pink tissue, and gently placed them in a cute bag. I thanked her and quickly pushed the stroller to a nearby bench. There I freed Hannah from her tether and fed her juice and animal crackers. I dug her favorite stuffed seal from my backpack to play with while I dodged into a baby store and purchased several onesies along with a soft blanket for the shower. We made it to the parking lot before she erupted again.

Later that night, after the kids were finally in bed, I cleared my underwear drawer of the old granny styles and deposited them unceremoniously in the trash can. Jake and Ellie eyed them eagerly; I put the receptacle on the mud porch so they couldn't retrieve them. Then I gently removed my new treasures from their tissue, carefully snipped the price tag from each one, and placed them gently in the drawer. They were beautiful and made of fine cotton with wide waistbands and sturdy elastic. No more underwear sneak for me.

The next morning, I noticed a difference in my attitude as I pulled on my buttery soft bikini. I felt confident, a little bit sexy, and even managed to fit in a yoga session that afternoon (plank position was a great workout with three kids hanging on me). From then on, those panties lifted my spirits as I chopped thistles, canned spaghetti sauce, entertained three small tyrants, and cleaned up after naughty canines. Choosing the pattern or color of the day was something I looked forward to. Polka dots brightened gloomy days and floral patterns heralded spring. I unabashedly raised the underwear bar when my pretty panties fluttered on our laundry line.

I officially became an underwear junkie. Stray couch and van coins funded my underwear addiction; it was surprising how much they amounted to in a short span of time. The flattering new styles made me feel better about my body than I had in years and provided a happy launch into my nonstop-a-million-things-to-do country days.

Chapter 22

THE GRAVEL LANE CONNECTING OUR HOUSE and sheds to the road filled with teeth-rattling ruts after every heavy rainfall. Raking them out wasn't a horrible job, but I really didn't need extra arm workouts on top of all the thistle chopping I was doing. The weeds were fronting a strong offense again. I had won the first battle but was in danger of losing the war. Our neighbors employed a tractor to mow weeds into submission and grade their driveways. We needed one too.

Alex, Amie, Hannah, and I wandered through rows of heavy machines at a large implement dealer. The shiny new models were far from our financial reach, but there were affordable options in the back of the lot. A vision danced in my head of our land transformed into tall grass stands dotted with prairie flowers and groves of mighty red oak tree. We would skip to the creek on wide paths with picnic baskets of fried chicken and red checked tablecloths instead of being attacked by purple-headed-monster thistles.

A salesman patted the engine on a 1940 gray Ford 9N. "This one is perfect for you," he stated. Wheels taller than me balanced with smaller ones in front, allowing it to traverse hilly land with ease. Wide fenders on each side tapered toward the back, where a wicked-looking PTO shaft spun to operate a blade and mower. I wrote the check before anyone else claimed our machine; it was delivered one sizzling Saturday when you could feel the corn leaves withering in the hot, dry breeze.

All of us crowded around our newest acquisition, arguing over who received the privilege to sit in the curved metal seat first. I lost; in a flash Alex grinned down at me from his perch. After his turn, I hooked it up to our small wooden wagon we had purchased from a neighbor and hauled three grinning kids up and down the gravel road.

On Sunday, Ken showed me how to hitch the tractor to a brush hog that housed three deadly spinning blades. He sternly instructed me to stay clear of the quickly spinning power takeoff shaft that ran the mower. No reminder needed; I preferred my appendages intact. Becky blew bubbles with the kids as I bounced along the fence line down to the pasture. Once I activated the mower, I carefully guided my new machine between the rows of red twig dogwoods, river birches, and swamp oaks. After an hour of mowing, beheaded silver weeds, Canadian thistles, and shredded red root plants littered the ground. Our young trees and shrubs had room to spread and grow. My shoulders and arms were grateful. I was in love.

There was one problem with the object of my affection. It was a moody machine. Occasionally the engine just seized up, jolting the tractor and whoever was on it to a dead stop. The first time it happened, our salesman dropped by in response to my panicked call. He rubbed the stubble on his chin thoughtfully as he examined the grey hunk of metal stalled in the middle of our lane. Pulling a heavy chain from the bed of his rusty pick up, he hooked up the front axle of our tractor to the rear axle of his truck. While he slowly dragged the tractor forward, I pushed in the clutch and turned the key. The engine coughed to life. It didn't happen very often, but whenever our tractor dug its wheels in and refused to move, I left it and called the salesman who lived nearby. After a few days he would stop by to resuscitate our little Ford.

Alex helped me grade our lane with a blade attachment. My son and I both sat on the curved metal seat as he steered, and I operated the brake and accelerator. It only took us thirty minutes to level that gravel; manual raking would have taken me days to accomplish the same thing. It was good for him to learn rudimentary driving skills with just one speed of slow. He never crashed the tractor, but I still planned on buying the children helmets when they started driving cars. Mangled images of the picket fence after repeated collisions with their plastic vehicles still haunted my dreams.

One weekend I hitched the tractor up to our little wooden wagon. The kids bounced up and down on their hay bales, ready to go. The gas gauge hovered near "E," so I grabbed one of the plastic gasoline containers off the machine shed bench, twisted the cap off the engine, and tried not to breathe in the fumes as I filled the tank. Then we set off for the fire lane near our house. We had just turned around when I noticed vapor hissing from the hood. That was new. By the time we parked near the barn, thick white steam shrouded the tractor. I sent the kids inside and wondered what was wrong this time. Swinging the engine compartment open, I peered through the gasoline-scented fog at the mass of wires, metal lines, and spark plugs. Then I realized I had mistakenly put gasoline into the radiator instead of the actual gas tank.

My neighbor Ken graciously hid his laughter when he arrived after receiving my urgent phone call for help. The tractor had stopped smoking. Sure enough, after Ken opened the radiator cap, gasoline fumes assaulted our noses. He scratched his head for a moment as I twisted the rag I held in my hands. Had I killed our beloved machine? But Ken came up with a simple solution. Water was denser than gas. If we flushed the radiator's tiny metal chambers, the fuel would be displaced.

I attached a hose to the outside pump, turned the water on, and stuck it inside the radiator. While Ken monitored our set up, I ran inside to check on the kids and give them a snack. It took over an hour to clean the intricate grates, but finally the water going into the radiator smelled the same as the liquid coming back out. Then Ken helped me fill the radiator with new antifreeze. I crossed my fingers and turned the key. The engine stuttered, coughed, and then purred like a cat. I thanked Ken profusely as he grinned and climbed back into this car. I painted the radiator reservoir lid with fire engine red nail polish so I wouldn't make the same mistake again.

Sitting on that cold metal tractor seat gave me a different perspective of our land. I decided to mow a new path one afternoon while Becky was babysitting. Something different from the usual patches of milkweed and wild pink roses was growing along the fence lines. Long blue vines reached toward the sun along single-track deer paths. I shut the tractor off, jumped when it backfired, dismounted with a pounding heart, and walked up to the plants. They were wild black raspberry vines, loaded with plump fruit. I popped a few in my mouth, then made a hasty retreat. The mosquitoes hovering in the shade were hungry. I killed five on my arm with one slap of a hand.

I drove the tractor back to the shed, ran into the house, doused myself with insect repellant, and changed into long pants and sleeves. The kids begged to come along, but I sent them to the garden to pick red raspberries with Becky instead. Less bugs there. Clyde and I hiked back down to the vines. Despite my fortified defenses, the mosquitos continued to attack. When my ice cream bucket was full, I ran from the bushes into the sunshine and hopped in the creek to sooth my itchy legs and arms in the cold water. Then I followed Clyde's waving tail back to the farmhouse where my crew was eating all the raspberries they had picked. Becky told me her mom was making a batch of jam with the wild black raspberries harvested from their thickets that afternoon. I dug through the freezer for my last bucket of vanilla ice cream, scooped some into bowls, and sprinkled the freshly picked berries on top. As we sat on the front porch steps guarding our dishes from the dogs and cats, I was again thankful for our new lives-- even though I had lost a significant amount of blood for our dessert.

I purchased a stronger insect repellent. It worked longer than the first spray, but I still had to deal with the vine's brutal thorns. Body armor would have been better. But those outings acquainted me with some of the wildlife that was re-establishing itself in our pasture now that the cows were gone. A doe, her dappled fawn, and I surprised each other one day as I strolled along one of the paths. All three of us stood motionless until Clyde bounded into view. Then both deer wheeled, flipped their white tails up and leaped over the sagging fence. Another time my ears picked up a buzzing noise that wasn't a high-pitched mosquito whine. I tracked the noise to honeybees gathering pollen on a nearby wild rose. I watched in fascination until one flew right past my nose and into a huge beehive on a branch of a gnarled hawthorn hanging directly over my head. I panicked, turned around, and ran through the brush back to my starting point as fast as I could. Luckily the bees didn't care about my trespassing, and I only lost a few berries.

The summer passed quickly. Before I knew it, I was sitting on the front porch labeling school supplies for Alex and Amie. Amie could barely contain her excitement for preschool, and Alex was enrolled in first grade. It was just Hannah and me home during my days off from the store. It was only Hannah and I at home on my days off, and strangely peaceful in the house with just the two of us. We read books, painted pictures together, and picked tomatoes and red raspberries. She became my sous chef during canning season. I began to wonder what life was going to be like when all three of them were in school. I did not have much time to ponder though.

Jake had returned from his frolic through the neighborhood and slunk up the porch steps where Hannah and I awaited the school bus. Eau de fresh skunk made both our eyes burn; I ran inside to grab dog shampoo.

Chapter 23

I WANTED MY KIDS TO GROW UP with fond memories of their lives in the country. Preserving foods, drying laundry on the line, occasional road trips, and hayrides behind the tractor had already become ingrained into our daily lives. But I yearned for more traditions to firmly root us. After sniffling through too many Hallmark movies that the whispering voice insisted on watching, I decided family reunions, county fair visits, and a holiday open house would create those memories.

An elderly aunt had been the driving force for my childhood family reunions. Her annual gatherings delivered happy memories of eating and playing with cousins, followed by fireworks at night. But she moved to Montana, and the reunions ended. Reviving them sounded like a fun thing to do. Our farm had plenty of room for hosting summer soirees. My family and distant relatives could reconnect, eat homecooked food, and play baseball. No fireworks though; a fire in our neighbor's bean fields would be bad.

The week before our first reunion, the old John Deere mower we imported from the suburbs died. It sat in a repair shop while our front yard softball diamond succumbed to tall clover and scraggly grass. I didn't have time to weed the gardens. On the day of the party, our farm was hardly the manicured grounds of my vision. As our guests arrived, Jake and Ellie devoured an entire plate of blonde brownies left unattended on the dining room table. Clyde made off with half a roasted chicken cooling on the stove. My favorite uncle got tipsy from his homemade dandelion wine. And a peaceful croquet game escalated to a mallet fight between Alex, Amie, and Hannah. Despite the mishaps (which made the inaugural reunion even more memorable), everyone had a good time and vowed to return every year after.

    Attending the county fair was another wonderful country tradition I had grown up with. I wanted the same for my kids. The August week-long event showcased tractor pulls, horse shows, musical acts, demolition derbies, and a midway lined with amusement rides and games to win stuffed animals. Young farmers competed against each other with livestock, homegrown vegetables, and grains. Fair judges (mostly from the county extension office which was a resource for landowners) sampled pies, preserves, and cakes and handed out blue ribbons while 4-H kids exhibited their summer projects.

    In my youth, my best friend and I wandered the livestock barns and rode amusement rides until we were dizzy. We didn't care so much about the cows and sheep; it was the cute boys we batted our eyes at. One time I had the bright idea of jumping a fence to bypass the entrance and its fees so we could save our money for fried cheese curds. My friend hopped the fence gracefully; she was the track high jumper. When I swung my second leg over the top strand, my blue jeans snagged on a fence barb. I froze, delicately balanced, and tugged. No release. My friend frantically motioned me forward as she crouched beside a muddy truck; the mounted patrol was approaching. I kicked hard until the material came free with a ripping sound, landed on the other side, and raced over to where she hid. We stifled our giggles until we were sure the guards passed. But when I explained to my parents the reason for my ruined pants later that night, I was told to buy my own replacement pair-- five times more expensive than fair admission. And my mother stood behind me as I blushed and handed over all my babysitting money to enter the grounds the next day.

Visiting the county fair was a different experience as a mom. Hopping fences to evade admission fees was not an option. I needed to be a good example for my children, not a fugitive. Plus, the stroller was too heavy to hoist. Instead of sauntering from building-to-building batting eyes at potential suitors, I spent most of my time in the implement area retrieving children from various combines and tractors. No one wanted to flirt with an exhausted mom pushing a stroller containing two whining little girls while gripping the hand of a five-year-old.

Touring the livestock barns was the only way I could make them all happy. Greedy goats nibbled at our fingers when we scratched between their ears. Gentle black and white Holsteins and brown Jerseys lumbered meekly behind their owners to and from the show rings. Exotic breeds of chickens and ducks squawked and quacked inside their wire crates along aisles of the fowl building. We admired displays for each local farm that held pictures of prize steers and milking cows, along with bunking areas for the kids who slept in the barns with their livestock and played tricks on each other all night.

Our final grand country tradition was a December holiday open house. After I spent early Thanksgiving morning hours peeling potatoes, mixing a green bean casserole, and digging out the heart, liver, and bony neck from the cavity of a hapless bird. I ignored the stacks of dirty pans and dishes swimming in soapy water. While my family dreamed their way through a turkey stupor, I dragged bins of Christmas decorations down from the attic. By the time the kids woke, tiny white lights twinkled from our dining room shelves, kitchen windows, and doorways. Our countdown to the big date was on.

Following the baking schedule scribbled on the refrigerator calendar, the kids and I mixed, baked, and frosted different sweets in preparation for the party. The first year Alex created a counter construction site after we cut out sugar cookies. Using his miniature die-cast tractors and bulldozers, he mounded and leveled the left-over flour into an imaginary gravel pit. When he did not share a front-end loader with Amie, she retaliated with white handprints on his shirt. The fight escalated to flying flour until I declared a truce between sneezes.

The winter gathering gave me an opportunity to visit with friends and neighbors. At least until I had to dash off after one of the dogs who snagged a crescent-roll-wrapped wiener again. Amie and Hannah, dressed in green velvet dresses, were tasked with keeping sugar cookie and fudge platters full. They probably ate as much as they served. Alex picked up used cups and plates before Ellie or Jake seized the chance to slurp up the leftovers. The merriment got rather wild with loud music, singing, and dancing the first year: my children wandered downstairs at two in the morning and sternly instructed all the adults to "to turn that crap down" so they could sleep.

Those new traditions created lasting memories. I loved that our farmhouse converted easily from holiday parties to filling station for summer water balloons. I was not disappointed that our farm gatherings did not crystallize into the poignant scenarios I had imagined. The food was sometimes burnt, and our grounds, dogs, and children were seldom tame. But in our fast-paced, crazy world where everyone was busy being busy, I hoped Running Horse Farm provided family and friends with warm memories where everyone was welcome and there was always a crowd in the kitchen.

Chapter 24

OUR SOLE LANDSCAPING FEATURE was a rusted livestock watering tank that squatted in the middle of our front yard. Previous owners had filled it with dirt and a few scraggly petunias, but weeds had taken over. Now that we were experienced horticulturists (with the vegetable garden and fledgling forest), I decided to dive into a little outside decoration. Besides addressing the ugly flower planter, something was needed around the front porch posts to distract viewers from the bare clay around them and the dirty basement windows behind them.

    I envied homes that had beautiful gardens, where varieties of flowers in a rainbow of colors bloomed through every season. I did not possess the time, energy, or talent to develop those, so I waited for an idea to arrive. One day as Hannah and I sat on the porch swing watching a turkey vulture circle slowly over the fields, I noticed orange lilies blooming in the ditch across the road. They were prolific and resilient. Perfect for a low maintenance flower garden.

    Beginning my beautification effort beneath our new white porch rails seemed the most logical choice. One morning, after banging a milk shed window back into its frame, I gathered my gardening tools. Hannah offered to help, but there was a new batch of kittens to play with. She made a good choice. I used a shovel to try to loosen the earth along the posts. A hammer and chisel would have more efficient. The dirt was as hard as granite.

I took a break to capture a kitten for Hannah and guzzled cold water from the hose. Then I returned to my dig site. An hour of back-breaking labor netted me a shallow trench along the porch. Good enough to start with. I trundled the wheelbarrow over to the other side of the road and began to uproot lilies. The ditch released them without a fight; its soil was a wonderfully loose mixture of gravel deposited by snowplows in the winter and rich black earth from the fields. Once I had a full load, I furtively looked both ways for traffic. Was there a law against removing wild plants from roadsides? I scanned once more for potential witnesses and trotted the heavy load back to the porch before the police arrived.

After parking my stolen plants by the little channel, I began placing them at intervals in the ground. Then I mounded loose dirt back around them and shooed Clyde away before he marked the flowers as his territory. The wobbly line of spiky greenish-yellow plants looked pathetic, but I knew they would take off if I remembered to water them.

Next, I tackled the livestock tank. It was heavy. I pulled so hard that I fell backward into the crabgrass, while the tank smirked at my feeble efforts. It refused to budge after thirty minutes of sweat and choice words. So, I emptied the dirt out and put it around the lilies that Hannah had just finished watering. Once the aluminum tank was empty, I swung it back and forth across the lane. Pausing at the metal pasture gate to catch my breath, I unlatched the panel and pushed the tank through. The metal made a horrible shrieking sound on the cement yard. After a lot of wiggling, grunting, and bad words, I left it in a deep gully where it could rust in peace.

The transplants underneath the front porch sent up new green shoots after six days. Encouraged by that success, I thought some of our other buildings might benefit from a little sprucing up too. After a few weeks, there were nice borders of flowers around the north side of the barn and milk shed. They needed edging, but the plastic ones we'd used in the suburbs were expensive. I waited for inspiration to strike and worked on another mural instead.

Before I drove to the health food store one morning, I walked down to the tree pasture with my cutter. There were a few thistles that had escaped the tractor, and I wanted to chop them before they seeded. They fell easily to my swings; maybe I was getting stronger. Or maybe they missed their friends. As I walked back up along the fence line, I stumbled over a limestone rock in the path. There were many partially unearthed stones spread throughout our paddock and forest land. They were a menace, and I was constantly warning the kids to not trip over them. That night, just before I fell asleep, I realized that those stones would make great borders for my gardens. And they were free.

The kids and I began scouting for rocks every time we hiked to the creek. We placed our finds in small piles. When I had spare time, I hauled them back to the gardens in a cart hitched to our four-wheeler. The limestone borders gave a very natural look to all my stolen plants, and I was always on the lookout for more landscaping material. There was a large, jumbled mass of cement slabs piled next to the barn, and I pondered how I could break them into useable pieces.

We hadn't seen many snakes on our farm, but that pile seemed like a perfect home for them. Even though reptiles ate mice and rats, I really didn't want a bunch of them slithering rampant on our property. While Jody, Terry and I stitched our wall hangings one evening, I shared my idea to break the big pieces into smaller ones and use them for garden borders. Ken overheard and said he had just the right tool for the job. He drove over the next day with an iron pipe filled with lead.

Ken lifted the pipe from his car like it was a toothpick and carried it over to the pile. He lifted the pipe up and smashed the end down on the center of his target. The cement slab broke obediently into small pieces. My turn. I dragged the heavy pipe to another slab, feebly lifted the pipe up and lowered it. Nothing. I grinned sheepishly at Ken. Apparently, some muscle was required. Summoning my thistle-cutting-biceps, I gave the piece a few stronger whacks. Encouraged by the tiny crack that appeared, I heaved the pipe one more time down onto the center, and grinned as it shattered. Soon there was a big pile of small irregular cement pieces perfect for garden edging. It was satisfying work. I waited a few days to move them, hoping any remaining snakes had plenty of time to find new homes.

Flowers, limestone rocks, and recycled cement became our farm's inexpensive and carefree landscaping. Our view was greatly enhanced by the lilies around the buildings and porch. Tulips and gladiolas replaced the old livestock tank. My gardens were not fancy but added a lot to our farm's curb appeal. And gave us more places to hurdle during our impromptu water fights.

Chicken Strips

Chapter 25

EVEN AFTER SEVERAL YEARS of what seemed like non-stop working on all the buildings, knee-deep ancient manure still occupied the bottom level of the barn, and the lean-to roof over the barn continued to ripple over rotted beams like a wind-swept ocean. I had officially completed every task on the list of "Potential Deadly Hazards," but the other lists had grown exponentially. It seemed like every time I checked off an item, another took its place.

Alex, Amie, and Hannah were growing rapidly; their height marks penciled on the kitchen doorframe leapfrogged upward every six months. Balancing work, parenting, and farm maintenance was a struggle. Losing sight of the truly important things, like spending time with the kids, was a constant danger. I put many projects on permanent hold. We had put down roots in the middle of nowhere, and it was time to become a contributing member of our new community.

Several moms who had kids in Alex's class recommended we start attending high school events. After our first Friday night football game, we were hooked. I hung out with the other parents as my children ran within the fenced field with their friends. I was a little hesitant at first but then realized any questionable behavior would be reported along with the guilty party. Alex, Amie, and Hannah looked forward to those evenings as a golden opportunity to devour fistfuls of concession candy and play tag.

Alex was in second grade, and his teacher was doing a wonderful job of helping him overcome his chronic shyness. Amie loved her all-day kindergarten, and Hannah was still home with me when I wasn't working. One afternoon, I found a meeting notice for the parent-teacher organization in Amie's and Alex's backpacks. Scribbling a note to myself, I taped it to the refrigerator between crayon stick figure drawings and marked it on my calendar.

I was able to escape child-free for the meeting but not without a struggle. Alex and Amie were fighting over what books Becky would read on the couch, and Hannah sobbed and clung to my leg as I tried to walk out the door. Becky pried her off, distracted her with a stuffed chicken, and agreed to read a book for each of them so I could run to the van. Terry's daughter, now a senior in high school, had become a very capable babysitter. I recognized a few faces when I walked into the cafeteria and grabbed an empty seat at a table with my football friends. Gazing at the typed agenda, I suddenly remembered how much I had disliked meetings when I worked in research. I squirmed in the little plastic chair but resolved to stay in the interest of my children's future.

The elementary school playground was addressed after minutes from prior meetings were read. It desperately needed updating; there had been money specifically designated for that purpose from the previous year's fundraising profits. A volunteer to lead the project had not been identified. My hand floated up before I could stop it and captured the position of project chairman.

Unlike the sleekly plastic modern recreation facilities we had frequented in the suburbs, the Orangeville playground equipment showcased old metal. The tall aluminum slides had inadequate rails on the top platforms. Metal monkey bars occupied the center of the area, a perfect concussion opportunity for my children even though I had once loved hanging upside down from their cold thin traverses. Finally, a wooden merry-go-round squatted menacingly in the northern corner. I remembered my friends and I pushing a similar model at a park to a satisfactory speed, jumping on and dangling from the iron rails at the edge until we could not walk straight. Now visions of plaster casts on young limbs danced in my head.

I decided to approach our project scientifically. The project leadership skills and management training I had learned during my corporate career finally came in handy. First, I requested information on governmental safety requirements. The detailed document that arrived in the mail several weeks later took effort to read through (it turned out to be a great sleep aid).

The next step was to identify new items that would provide a good play experience for children of all ages. I decided to evaluate different school playgrounds in our county, not only for their equipment but also their layouts. Alex, Amie, and Hannah explored a new park each weekend while I took notes and photographs. It was the most fun I'd ever had during the research phase.

According to the safety guidelines, we needed to get rid of everything except for two sets of swings and a wooden climbing structure at the southern end. There was plenty of space to fill. After our playground reviews, the kids and I spent hours poring over equipment brochures to find items we thought would be a good fit. I often walked into the living room to find Amie and Hannah paging through the catalogs.

As we narrowed the options down, one company stood apart from the rest to fill our needs. We drafted a wish list and gathered a group of parents to make the final decision on what we would purchase. In that meeting, we chose seven different items that fit the budget and would provide a good mix of play opportunities. Our official report included the safety requirements according to government guidelines, a list of the equipment that needed to be removed, and the layout plan for the new items. I presented our proposal to the PTO who unanimously approved it. Then we approached the school board with our plan who joined in the approval as well. Word about the project spread quickly throughout town, and several families volunteered to adopt the old slides, monkey bars, and merry-go-round.

We placed our order and garnered a spot in the school bus garage to store the huge packages when they arrived. One of my PTO friends dove into organizing the official playground-raising. She coaxed food from our local grocer and found people to operate the construction equipment we needed. The kids and I put posters up around town to entice even more help.

The designated day dawned cool but sunny. I was relieved: rain would have delayed digging holes and setting foundations for the posts. Becky had offered to watch the kids during construction; she bravely faced the band set-up the kids had arranged in the living room. All the dogs were hiding from the loud drumming and pretend guitars under my bed.

As volunteers filtered in, honorary construction foremen briefed different crews and pored over equipment assembly instructions. Donated food was placed in the shelter house to fuel everyone. I brought my infamous raspberry coffee cake (it disappeared in two minutes!) Most of the men congregated around a backhoe, setting anchor posts with cement. I marveled how heavy equipment always seemed to draw testosterone to it. Other volunteers began to assemble some of the smaller pieces. Intimidated by the large power tools required for assembly steps, I ventured over to the painting group at the swings. We needed a ladder to reach the tall parts, so I made a quick trip back to the farm to retrieve one.

I set the extension ladder against the main support for the swings and climbed up with a plastic cup containing paint and a brush. Smiling from my perch, I applied blue enamel onto the rusty iron. I had a bird's eye view of a community working together. Laughter and good-natured teasing filled the air around me as friends and neighbors labored side by side. After the structures were assembled, we raked truckloads of delivered mulch around and beneath each piece of equipment. By the end of the day, we had a beautiful new play zone for everyone to enjoy.

Every time I drove past our new grade school playground, I saw more than just a colorful area for children to laugh and run in. I remember a group of adults who cared very much about their community and its future. Helping redesign and raise that elementary playground was the beginning of my history in the small town I was proud to call home.

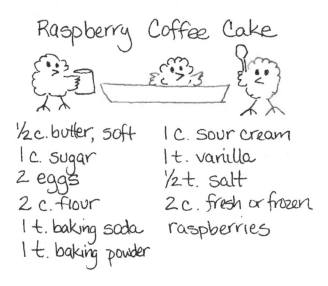

Raspberry Coffee Cake

½ c. butter, soft
1 c. sugar
2 eggs
2 c. flour
1 t. baking soda
1 t. baking powder

1 c. sour cream
1 t. vanilla
½ t. salt
2 c. fresh or frozen raspberries

Preheat oven at 350°. Grease 13x9 pan. Mix butter, sour cream, vanilla, salt, baking soda & powder, flour, eggs & sugar. Spread half in pan, top with raspberries. Spoon rest of batter over that. Then mix ½ c. sugar & ½ c. brown sugar — sprinkle this over everything. Bake for 30 min.

Chapter 26

WHEN I WAS EIGHT YEARS OLD, I badgered my parents until they bought me a pony. That little blonde gelding and I were inseparable from the moment we met. His soft whicker greeted me in the morning when I opened the shed door, and his velvety muzzle tickled my neck when I hugged him good night. Nuzzle snatched apples from stunted trees growing along the fence lines where we rode, and grazed on patches of long green grass as I led him around our yard. I spent hours brushing his coat, combing his tail, and braiding his mane. He was the keeper of all my secrets and dreams… my first love.

When I started high school, our life together changed. My pony spent more and more hours alone in his shed as I became consumed with homework and teenage angst. He had been a faithful friend and deserved someone new who had time to enjoy his companionship. I waved goodbye through a haze of tears as his sturdy rump bounced away in his new owner's trailer. I missed his friendship greatly and vowed that someday I would rekindle that wonderful romance. Our farm was my golden opportunity.

Our children were finally old enough that they were not in constant mortal danger if I kept the machine shed doors closed. With Becky as our babysitter, I had windows of opportunity where I could pursue a hobby of my own. The search for a family horse was on. My requirements were that it be a gentle and docile gelding. That was a tall order for twelve hundred pounds of flesh governed by a tiny steel bit. I did not want anything too fast, too spooky, too young, or too spirited. But bomb-proof horses were rare. It was risky buying a mount at one of the local sale barns, so I made a few phone calls and put the word out on the country grapevine. Just when I was ready to give up the search and spend another summer cantering through fields in my dreams, a nearby livestock owner called. They had several horses for sale, and one was a sweet palomino who followed me around like a puppy. When I gazed into his calm brown eyes, I knew he was the one.

After I arranged to have him delivered, I drove the kids to our farm supply store. We spent hours in the horse aisle picking out all the essentials: hoof picks, curry comb brush, lead ropes, a bridle, and fly spray. The neighbors hauled their cows away and cleaned out the cattle shed to make room for him. On the day he was scheduled to arrive, we watched the road for telltale dust. As the truck and trailer pulled into our lane, Alex, Amie, and Hannah hovered behind me. My golden horse backed out of the trailer with a noisy clatter of hooves and looked at us curiously. His old owner placed the halter lead in my shaky hands and wished me luck.

Instantly my brain turned to mush. I felt totally helpless with a massive animal at the other end of the rope. Luckily, he was a very patient horse and greedily chewed the un-mowed grass while I contemplated how to get him into the paddock. I shortened the lead and gave him a gentle tug. He lifted his head and quietly followed me through the gate. After I unsnapped the rope, he sedately wandered around the area and stopped to graze a patch of purple clover. The kids and I stood on the metal gate's bottom rung to admire his pretty head and burnished copper coat. We named him "Blaze" for the wide stripe of white that traveled from his eyes to his nose.

I let Blaze settle into his new surroundings for a few days before beginning what I hoped would be a wonderful relationship. But my attempts at catching him were futile, even though he still wore a halter. He had plenty to eat and was not about to be lured in by the handful of grain I pleadingly offered. I asked a neighbor who had several horses for help. She showed me how to walk slowly up to him with the rope over my shoulder, talking softly the whole time to distract him, and quietly put the lead around his neck. Her method worked well. All lists were forgotten. I spent spare hours grooming my yellow horse and getting to know the areas he liked having scratched.

After a week of bonding, I turned my horse out into the larger paddock. Watching him gallop around the fence line with his tail held high made my heart expand with pride. But there he had more room to evade me. Sometimes catching Blaze consumed every spare minute, so I returned to the farm supply store and purchased butterscotch treats. After the first taste, he was addicted and allowed me to halter him as long as I had plenty of the nuggets in the pockets of my blue jeans.

After grooming him one day, I dragged the heavy saddle I'd purchased to the gate. Blaze's ears swiveled forward immediately. I smoothed a heavy blanket over his broad back, then heaved the saddle on top of that. My horse stood like a statue through my fumbling with the girth and cinches, occasionally swatting me with his tail. He willingly accepted the bridle and bit as I pulled the soft leather straps gently over his ears and hooked the chin piece in place.

The kids stood on the metal gate as I prepared to mount. The saddle seemed solid when I rocked it slightly. Drawing a deep breath, I put my left foot in the stirrup and tried to swing my other foot up and over. No luck. His back was a lot further from the ground than I thought. Alex, Amie, and Hannah snickered. My second attempt was just as gracefully unsuccessful, and the kids almost fell off the gate laughing. Finally, on the third try, I jumped as high as I could and landed with my stomach on the saddle. Wiggling my right leg over to the other side, I poked my foot around until it rested in the stirrup and settled into the rounded leather seat. Blaze turned his head to stare at me, shocked that I had actually made it. I gathered the reins in one hand, held the saddle horn in the other, and gently nudged his sides with my heels.

As we slowly walked in a circle, the old familiar thrill of being astride a horse immediately coursed through me. With a huge smile on my face, I steered him into the big paddock. His gait gently rocked me as we ambled through the grass. I was in heaven and became lost in time until the kids' voices floated toward me. Words of "hungry" and "thirsty" jolted me back to reality. I turned Blaze back toward the shed and stroked his neck happily; our first ride had been a success! After I removed his bridle and saddle, he trotted to a patch of bare dirt, buckled at the knees and rolled back and forth on the ground. Then he scrambled to his feet, shook the dust off, and thundered as far away as he could get.

After that initial ride, I spent much of my spare time either chasing my horse down or bouncing on his broad back. While Becky watched my kids, I trotted him in circles and cantered in figure eights inside our paddock until I felt confident with my skills. Soon we ventured out into our neighborhood. Leaves rustled softly above us as we walked along the fire lane and gravel roads. Thousands of little yellow butterflies fluttered around us as we cantered in figure eights in Ken's alfalfa fields. I reveled in the seductive smell of horse sweat laced with leather and spent so many hours in the saddle that permanent sores scabbed over inside both my knees. I was so happy to have rekindled my dream of equine romance. But just like every sport, horseback riding was not without peril. He was a tall horse, and I learned one day how distant I was from the ground. I remember hearing the birds chattering in trees, gathering for migration. Blaze and I galloped through tall grasses on a forest preserve trail when he suddenly spooked and shied to the right. I catapulted over his ears and landed headfirst on the ground with one foot still tangled in the stirrup. I fought the stars circling my head and managed to shake my foot free. Staggering to my feet, I held the reins tight and soothed my horse as he fidgeted around me. Everything moved in slow motion. Once he was still, I gingerly climbed back into the saddle.

Blaze and I were both jumpy as we headed home. There was no more racing. I held the saddle horn tightly in one hand, and a fistful of his mane with the reins in the other. Every step sent a wave of nauseating pain to my head and hip. Back home, after he was unsaddled and turned loose in the pasture, I limped to the house. Ice packs, hot baths and ibuprofen helped my minor concussion and bruises heal. My palomino received some well-deserved time off, and I re-acquainted myself with my children.

The second fall was less traumatic on my body, but more hurtful to my pride. I reached forward to brush some flies away from Blaze's face one day as we trotted along a path in our forest land. He interpreted that as a mountain lion attack and spun so quickly I flew over his shoulder. He cantered back to the shed with his tail held high. I trudged after him, grumbling about my bruised pride. He meekly stood still as I hopped back into the saddle. He needed to understand that I thought I was still the one in control.

Blaze became my trusted confidant and friend. He listened patiently to all my hopes and dreams as I combed his tail, cleaned his feet, and admired the countryside from his broad back. Blaze was not mean-spirited; he didn't intend to dump me like my childhood pony had. I just needed to become a better rider and anticipate his small brain's perceptions. He was everything I had hoped for in a one-ton hoofed companion.

Chapter 27

ONE OF THE CHALLENGES OF RAISING CHILDREN on a desolate gravel road was boredom. Boredom gave birth to whining. Whining raised my blood pressure, which led to a form of discipline known as find-something-to-do-or-I-will-give-you-work. Our three slunk into the shadows when my voice dropped to its dangerously low tone upon hearing about their terminal lack of anything fun to do. Alex, Amie, and Hannah had to discover ways to entertain each other.

In the summertime, there were plenty of books to read, dogs to walk, siblings to tease, and butterflies to catch. We had great front row seats for thunderstorms on our porch swing. Fireflies at dusk provided flickering fireworks in the fields all around us. But probably the one of the best hot weather activities was an old-fashioned water fight.

When the sun reached its zenith on scorching August days, icy water from the well remedied the heat. We set up a slip-n-slide on the barn hill where I learned that middle-aged moms probably should avoid diving onto the ground. My back didn't approve of my high center of gravity. But the kids sure had fun. And good old-fashioned water fights were always welcome. Our neighbors often surprised us with an ambush from the cornfields surrounding our house. We learned to maintain an arsenal of water balloons in buckets and loaded water guns placed in strategic places.

When the invaders' battle whoops erupted, we raced into the battlefield and grabbed whatever weapons we could find. I even kept a few water pistols by the kitchen sink, just in case. One battle escalated into the house with buckets and the hose; my out-of-control skid landed me face to face with a solid pine door. The war was waged outside after that. The best part was after our battles; all participants met on the front porch to eat popsicles peacefully together.

My father acquired a small sailboat one year and needed a place to store it. We had plenty of room, so it found a home in our machine shed. One morning Alex and I decided to haul it out into the yard. We dusted it off, set up the boom and mast, and practiced our boating skills. When the breeze snapped the sail, I showed him how to tack to avoid getting whacked overboard. The next day he recruited Amie and Hannah to be shipmates. They spent hours exploring their imaginary ocean, visiting new lands, and braving the mighty waves.

When cold winds whistled through the windows of our Victorian farmhouse, water fights, Barn Town, and sailing the green lawn were replaced with sledding down the barn hill and skating on the frozen creek. If the danger of frostbite was imminent, we looked indoors for other options. Jake had chewed most of the little pieces in our board games, and none of us truly enjoyed puzzles. Alex, Amie, and Hannah built blanket forts in the living room. Occasionally, their boisterous inventions led to the sound of something shattering, followed by heavy silence. Then three young voices volunteered names of the responsible parties: Not Me and I Don't Know.

Folding the mountain of laundry always hovering in the corner of my bedroom gave rise to several activities. Besides the obvious using-the-bed-as-a-trampoline, sock wars were fun and a lot safer. After rolling socks up into balls, we divided piles between players. From behind doorways, we hurled them at each other, scoring points for direct hits. No one was ever hurt by this game, unless you counted bruises from diving onto hardwood floors as we avoided the bombs. A variation of that game was dubbed "panty palooza." Clean underwear was the weapon, and the goal was to land them on someone else's head. I found stray socks and underwear hidden in corners for years.

One particularly long February day, desperation sent us searching the attic to retrieve old toys. Train sets circled the dining room. The kids discovered an old drum set and plastic guitar hidden in the rafters and formed a rock band. It was a slight improvement over the pots, pans, and wooden spoons they had employed as toddlers. But apparently my children had inherited my lack of rhythm and tone deafness. I quietly moved their instruments up to "barn town" after I found the dogs hiding in a closet to escape the noise.

Well-loved but forgotten stuffed animals found new life as ammunition for blanket tent wars. The kids blocked light from the living room by placing towels over the windows and built bunkers out of couch cushions and pillows in corners. Like prairie dogs, Amie, Alex, and Hannah popped out of their burrows, dodging, tossing, and laughing.

Those imaginative times faded much too quickly as computer screens began luring my children into a new world of games. Stuffed animals and water guns slowly migrated to bins in the attic. Keyboard clicking replaced silliness and shrieking, unless it was a fight over whose turn it was. But I wasn't ready to relinquish those younger playful years just yet. At least weekly, I unplugged the electronics and took the kids up to the barn where we dusted off their vehicles, instruments, and playhouse and put them back to use. If the weather was too cold, we dragged the stuffed animals from their bins, covered the windows, and I joined them in prairie dog games.

The Rooster In the Drive Thru

Chicken Strips

Chapter 28

SWEAT DRIPPED DOWN MY BACK. I slapped a mosquito on my arm, leaving a bloody trail. "See what these escapes cost me?" I muttered at the black and white goat. Bits of wax bean seedlings dangled from his lips. I feigned left, dodged right, grabbed his head and held on tight until the rope was securely fastened around his neck. Then I tugged him back into the barn. Our goats had become adoptees with no tangible benefit. In exchange for their extremely comfortable lives, the bearded mammals escaped their prison-like eight strand electric fence to plunder my flower and vegetable gardens with abandon.

It all started when our neighbor downsized his milking herd. Literally. From dairy cows to cloven-hoofed little demons. He stopped by one day and invited Amie and Alex over to observe his operation. The goats were cute, friendly, and their small stature made them easily manageable. After the initial introduction to milking, my two grade schoolers were enamored with the fuzzy creatures.

Soon my late sleepers were leaving their beds at five in the morning in the summer months. They hopped aboard our four-wheeler and zoomed through the fields to help with our neighbor's chores. They herded goats from the pasture into the milking parlor and cleaned teats. They connected udders to pumps, collected the milk, and sent the relieved goats back out to the pasture. Then the next crew of mother goats were herded into the barn and the process repeated. But bottle feeding the greedy weaned babies was the highlight; Alex and Amie fought over who got to hold the plastic bottles outfitted with big rubber nipples. It was hard work, and when the kids returned to my farm, they were too exhausted to do anything but simply collapse on their beds and sleep all day.

After a month, Amie and Alex each received a young goat as a reward for their labor. Hershey and Lightning followed Alex and Amie like puppies and sucked greedily on their milk bottles. We set up a stall inside the lower level of our big barn for them, featuring a nice little ramp leading to a small pen outside. After we turned on the electric for the eight-strand fence (we'd been warned), we turned them loose to run merrily about the thistles and weeds. But their growth rate was astounding, and we realized we had miscalculated the amount of pasture they required. Within weeks they crunched all vegetation to nubs and began eyeing the green grass outside their pen hungrily.

Hershey and Lightning devoured everything within reach when they were on their ropes. They dragged Alex and Amie to my gardens, where we learned that they were actually picky eaters. They preferred only the finest of produce and flowers. Petunias, peppers, and Hosta plants were high on their delicacy list, as were my prize red raspberries. Banishing them back to their pen only left them bleating pitifully and eyeing the tomatoes.

A second pair of goats migrated to our farm after a few months. We now had the equivalent of a small petting zoo without the income. The new babies were clever and devised ingenious ways to escape their corral. Then one of our health food customers offered up another squatter. Word had spread about my inability to say no, especially if I knew the animal was destined for the butcher. Houdini lived up to his name. One day, as I was loading the kids (human) into the van for our weekly trip to town, I spied his small silhouette cavorting in the green grass outside the fence—the same fence that had just been fortified with extra high voltage. I knew because I'd been on the receiving end of that powerful jolt several times while weed whacking.

Cursing quietly under my breath, I drove back up the lane. Luring him near with the promise of feed in one hand and a rope behind my back, I grabbed him and half-carried, half-dragged his fifty-something pound body back to the pen. Alex unlocked the gate and deflected escape by the other goats while I shoved Houdini back inside. By the time I climbed back into the van, black goat hair covered my new shirt.

Glancing in my rear-view mirror as I drove away for the second time, I saw Houdini jumping the fence and bounding toward our newly planted granny smith apple tree.

Throughout the winter months, I grew tired of nagging Alex and Amie to feed and tend their animals. Then our neighbor sold his goat herd (I think he grew tired of rounding up his errant animals just like me) and returned to milking docile Guernsey and Brown Swiss dairy cows. When our cloven-hoofed little devils finally just busted down the electric fence and stripped all the spring buds off my pink rhododendrons for a herd frolic one day, I surrendered. After penning them back up in the barn, I placed an advertisement in the local newspaper offering them (the goats, not the children-- although I was tempted) at no charge to whoever wanted them.

We received many calls on the first day, some suspiciously carnivorous in nature. The winning proposal was from a farmer who promised to use them to graze invasive honeysuckle from his woods. Alex, Amie, Hannah, and I loaded Hershey and crew into our neighbor's livestock trailer the next week; he had kindly offered to deliver them to the new owner for us. Hershey nibbled on my shirt sleeve apologetically as Houdini made one last ditch effort to escape. We shut the door firmly as their horns butted the door. The trailer disappeared in a cloud of gravel dust over the hill. Another farm farewell. But I knew it was the right decision.

The lower level of our three-story barn became silent. No one bleated to have their foreheads scratched anymore. My gardens, shrubs, and raspberries began recovering from the goat ravages. I unplugged the electric fence, rolled it all up and stowed it in a dark corner of the machine shed just in case we needed it someday. The swinging goat door I had so carefully constructed stood slackly open on its one remaining hinge; empty buckets and a small mound of manure sat forgotten in the pen. Thistles and burdock reclaimed the outside pen after two weeks.

Our goats had been an eye-opening experiment in animal husbandry. They had taught us that innocent-seeming critters could be destructive, devious, and cost much more in expenses than their entertainment value was worth. My horse was different. Blaze's cost equation was offset by the joy I felt every time I rode him along country lanes or brushed burrs from his tail. And even though Jake, Ellie, and Clyde were exasperating at times, I couldn't imagine life without fuzzy canine bodies surrounding me on the couch.

There had to be other farm creatures that would offer some benefits instead of just increasing my anxiety and adversely affecting our budget. Hannah had begun lobbying to raise chickens. Alex and Amie joined her committee. They were small and kind of cute (the birds,  not the children-- my kids were downright adorable). After all, how much damage could fowl cause?

Chapter 29

I CHOKED BACK THE LUMP IN MY THROAT as I straightened Hannah's backpack and queried Alex and Amie about whether they had used their toothbrushes or just run them under water. The first official day of school for all three of them had arrived. My babies had transformed into full time grade school students. When the bus pulled to a stop at our driveway in a swirl of gravel dust, I waved brightly to all three of them and bit back tears as they headed up the bus steps and disappeared inside.

Time to mourn was a luxury I didn't have though; our business wasn't doing as well as it had initially. The economy was hurting. While the kids were learning how to read, write, and divide inside the elementary school brick walls, I tried different methods to increase sales. In-house nutrition counseling services, customer loyalty programs, and weekly prize baskets stemmed the losses a little. But as months flew by, I discovered that many people came to our store for advice, and then purchased less expensive products somewhere else.

A fellow pharmacist called me one unseasonably hot September Saturday. I grinned when he asked me what I'd been doing. Sweat dripped from my forehead as I carefully placed jars of ruby red tomatoes into the water bath while cradling the telephone between my ear and shoulder. Steam surrounded me as I glanced out the kitchen window; Alex, Amie, and Hannah chased each other with squirt guns through the scraggly grass on one of the last warm days before fall. Jake and Ellie nosed through tomato skins and seeds littered onto the faded blue and white kitchen linoleum. Clyde's brown eyes followed my movements, silently willing me to open the cookie jar and toss him one of the dog treats stored inside.

"Are you ready to come back to the real world yet?" my friend asked. I pondered my answer for a minute. Maybe it was time to give pharmacy a try. We could use the money. He needed coverage for vacation for two weeks. It would work if I found coverage for the health food store and someone to watch the kids after school. But my part-time childcare search was fruitless; local daycare providers were booked, and Becky was busy with sports and activities during her final year of high school.

I pored over our store's accounting ledgers weekly. Profits from our business were barely enough to fund basic living expenses for our family, dogs, and a horse. Insurance premiums and property taxes threatened to push us into ruin. Despite heavy advertising, radio spots on local stations, and private consultations, our store sales were on a steady decline. The economy was tanking and placing my country lifestyle in jeopardy.

One day, as I explained the benefits of standardized milk thistle to a customer, the bell on the front door jingled. A nicely dressed businessman walked in, and I sighed. Salesmen always found me an easy mark. But this one waited patiently until I finished making the transaction, and then introduced himself as a recruiter for a small chain of pharmacies. He had heard we had a pharmacist on staff and wanted to discuss career opportunities with me. They desperately needed someone to cover evening shifts in a nearby town. I warned him that I was rusty; it had been years since I had dispensed medications.

The man possessed excellent persuasion skills and charmed me into an interview with the pharmacy manager the following day. She asked when I could start. Becky found several evenings free during the week so she could watch the kids until Alex received his babysitting certification. I dug out my old white pharmacy coat and completed a bunch of continuing education courses gleaned from trade journals to refresh my knowledge.

It was a challenge to switch from holistic health practices and ideals to current Western medicine philosophies. Many new drugs had flooded the market since I had graduated from college. And most pharmacy customers did not want to be counseled on nutrition or healthy life practices. I had trouble keeping at the expected pharmacist tempo, even in the quieter evening hours. Each prescription deserved as much scrutiny I would give to one for my children.

Deciphering orders, answering one of six telephone lines, checking prescriptions for interactions, and counseling patients on how to take their medications filled my part-time evenings. Stress over our financial situation declined with regular paychecks, but my anxiety level skyrocketed. Mistakes were unacceptable. Many nights I awoke from a restless sleep in a panic, worried that I hadn't told a patient to take their antibiotic with food. I was exhausted trying to balance days at the health food store with nights at the pharmacy. There was no time for farm projects. Blaze stood idle in his corral and the paths through our forestry land were being overtaken by thistles and weeds again.

I drafted Alex, Amie, and Hannah for household chores. They were old enough to run the vacuum, clean the tub, and swipe wooden surfaces with a cloth instead of practicing cursive writing in the dust. We held a family meeting to outline my plan. I felt a glimmer of hope as some of the weight lifted off my shoulders. Then the fighting began. The girls despised scrubbing the toilet with a plastic brush, and Alex couldn't keep up with canine snout prints smudged on every window. Nothing was equal or fair, and the amount they were paid was not even close to what their friends received by simply folding towels.

After a few months, we all settled into a better rhythm. I regained my confidence and retail skills and was able to finish a shift without leaving ten annoying questions for my manager the next day. My pharmacy coworkers quickly became new friends. The kids found chores they excelled in without bickering. After Alex completed a Red Cross babysitting course, I felt more comfortable leaving them for short periods of time if Becky was unavailable. The girls helped even more by doing occasional loads of laundry and cooking simple dishes.

Working in a pharmacy pressure cooker wasn't easy, but some of my favorite memories were coming home after a busy night to be greeted at the mud porch door by my children. After I made my selections from their hand-drawn dinner menu, they served me a wonderful meal. Jake, Ellie, and Clyde hovered between the kitchen and dining room, ready to clean any spills (and there were quite a few). But I didn't mind. It was the beginning of a new, hopeful era for all of us.

Chapter 30

AS WE BECAME MORE INGRAINED into rural life, I realized that our farm supported other populations besides human, canine, and equine. Indigenous species like possums, racoons, mice, and insects had made their homes in corners and rafters of our outbuildings long before we moved in. I didn't mind co-existing with other species if they remained outside; we had plenty of room for everyone on twenty acres. But my hospitality to other creatures did not extend to the inside of our farmhouse.

Bugs were an integral part of the rural ecosystem. I knew many of them had important functions, like pollinating and assisting in returning organic material to the earth. Flies made their appearance every spring, sustained by plentiful varieties of country manure. With three young children and numerous dogs traipsing in and out the doors a minimum of one thousand times a day, hundreds of flies maneuvered their way inside to take up residence. So, I purchased old fashioned fly strips and hung them in strategic spots. The flies skillfully avoided the traps, but I didn't. After losing a few chunks of hair, I took down the remaining sticky tapes and returned to my trusty fly swatter.

Ticks patiently waited in the woods and tall grasses for suitable hosts to walk by, especially in the spring. The tiny hitchhikers were amazingly adept at locating targets. They often found a ride into the house on one of the dogs, and sometimes decided a human host was more desirable. Many a night I awoke to that scalp-crawling sensation and would lie awake until I finally plucked the invader from my head and flushed it down the toilet. After removing numerous bloated grey insects from Jake, Ellie and Clyde, I started using the once-a-month liquid medicine instead of flea collars. It worked so well I contemplated dotting some of the solution on my neck too.

Earwigs were nocturnal bugs with oversized pincers protruding from their segmented bodies. I had no idea what their function was, except to scare the heck out of us. An entire colony of those fun-loving creatures to the farm was imported with the suburban picket fence, and they quickly colonized around our house. Blood-curdling screams from Amie or Hannah would alert me when one of those insects managed to find a way into the bathroom again. They loved to lurk around the toilet. Several even managed to pinch me before I flushed them down into the septic system. Sometimes I had nightmares that they grew into gigantic sizes in the drainage field, crawled back into our house, and began taking over the world. Not a bad horror flick.

At least country bugs died off after the first few frosts. Not so for rodents. After field crops were harvested and the first October cold snap hit, a virtual parade of mice migrated into our home through foundation cracks. It was not uncommon to see a furry form dart across the kitchen floor when we turned on the lights. I didn't have the heart to kill them, so we baited live traps with gourmet cheese and placed them in strategic places. Whenever I discovered a captive, I released it near one of the tomcats hovering by the mud porch door. But the feline just watched the mouse scamper away and meowed plaintively for table scraps instead.

The mouse probably shared a hearty chuckle with his friends at the main burrow and added intelligence information to the control room of maps showing entry points into the farmhouse, good places to hide, and best locations for finding food. The cycle of entrapment, release, sharing classified data, and stealthily regaining entrance back into our home continued until the weather warmed enough for them to forage for food outside again.

One morning before school, I was summoned by the girls to dispatch a tiny rodent. I figured he was searching for his mother whom I had set free in the garden the evening before. The little guy was backed up against a table leg, catching his breath. There was a random shoe box on the counter, probably for a school project that wasn't red alert status yet. I grabbed it. When he made a run for it, I trapped him with the box and slipped a cookie sheet beneath the cardboard. Then I carried him outside and set him free to find his mom.

Blaze's sweet molasses feed and oats provided a fast-food drive-thru when mice grew weary of crumbs in the house. Even though I stored the grain in plastic bins, the lids didn't fit tightly. Hannah raced inside one morning after chores, breathlessly informing me that there were two mice running in circles on top of the oats. After throwing on boots, we all raced to the horse shed. The rodents cowered together, looking up at us with horrified beady brown eyes. My three kids begged to keep them as pets. I couldn't say no. I hadn't had coffee yet.

Amie and I placed some newspapers at the bottom of our old hamster cage, set up a water bottle, and put a small container of sweet feed inside. I donned gloves just in case the varmints had sharp teeth, gently scooped them out of the barrel and placed them in their new home. After securing the mesh lid before the quick critters organized an escape attempt, we carried them into the kitchen. Our captives looked terrified as they scanned the room from the counter. That was surprising because I'm sure they had seen the kitchen numerous times. Alex retrieved an empty toilet paper tube and dropped it in the cage. They immediately climbed inside and peeked out at us from each end.

The girls named them Bob and Lisa. We had no idea which was which, and if either of them was truly boy or girl. I lugged the cage up to the girls' room, believing earnest promises of how they would take care of them. During the first several weeks, the rodent antics captivated us all. Bob and Lisa constantly scuttled about their cage, testing and re-testing every corner and crevice for a potential gateway to freedom. The lid of the cage had several plastic doors where we could drop food or water in. When the crate began to smell ripe, I dragged it out on the front porch for cleaning. If they escaped out there, they could always read the maps at base camp and find their way back inside the house.

On one of my rare days off, I began cleaning in preparation for our annual holiday open house. As I cleared the clutter from Amie's dresser, I noticed that one of the hatches on the cage's lid was slightly askew. My heart pounded as I lifted it and poked under shredded newspaper mounds and peered inside the toilet paper tube. No rodents. Bob and Lisa were on jail break, and we were five days away from having fifty guests in our house. Granted, many of our friends lived in the country and were used to critters, but I did not want anyone hurting themselves by jumping up onto our kitchen chairs.

We did not capture either fugitive with aged cheddar in the live traps. The situation was becoming desperate. Two days before the party, I sadly set snap traps up behind the dresser in the girls' room hoping Bob and Lisa would go for the live ones upgraded with organic peanut butter. But later that night, when we were downstairs baking sugar cookies, we heard a loud crack. I went upstairs and returned with a lifeless body dangling from the trap. Amie screamed as I sadly threw Bob (or Lisa?) out to the tomcat lingering by the backdoor. The cat casually consumed the meal (it was a lot less work when the mouse was already dead), and pitifully cried for scraps after. We found the second corpse an hour later. I tossed that one to a different cat (she was a good mouser and deserved a free dinner).

As I placed luminaries along the sidewalk the night of our party, I took a quiet moment to send an apology to Bob and Lisa skyward. No more field mice as pets. Our holiday open house was pleasant and rodent-free.

Despite their diminutive size, bugs and mice were extremely powerful. They made us scream, run, or stand motionless in fear. I knew both will be around long after humans became extinct and would still carry on their important functions of sucking blood, foraging, scaring, and scurrying. But that didn't mean I had to surrender the farm to them. Just like the thistles, some of my battles with Mother Nature were never going to end. I just needed to maintain a healthy arsenal of fly swatters and mouse traps to keep the invaders at bay.

Hawkeye Bars

1 c. butter   1 c. brown sugar
½ c. sugar   ½ c. milk
2 c. crushed grahm crackers
1 c. butterscotch chips   1 c. semi-sweet chocolate chips
½ c. peanut butter   Club crackers

Line 13x9 pan with club crackers. Mix butter, sugars, milk, and grahm crackers in pan and gently boil for five minutes. Pour ½ mixture over crackers, layer more club crackers over that, pour rest of carmel over those, and finish with 3rd layer of crackers. Melt chips & peanut butter, spread on top & cool.

Chapter 31

HANNAH FINISHED HER ROOSTER PAINTING one afternoon as I worked on a sketch of Blaze. It was fun to watch her artistic endeavors, even though the table ended up wearing as much paint as the paper did. She inherited that from me. Our refrigerator door and kitchen walls were plastered with her bird art.

My children had grown more passionate about raising chickens. Their reasoning seemed solid. Eggs would provide income, the birds would eat the earwigs still out wandering our yard, and all three of my kids would clean the coop without whining. I knew better about the last promise but did agree we needed to use the barn for some kind of livestock.

Before officially giving in, I researched raising poultry to avoid the pitfalls we had encountered with the goat disaster. Lack of interest in shoveling manure, expensive fencing, and the loss of my valuable vegetable crops had all been significant issues. From what I had researched, chickens sounded like a lot less work. Plus, they couldn't possibly produce as much poop as the goats had.

I knew surrendering to the pleas of my children meant I would most likely be the responsible caretaking party. But chickens and their eggs might contribute something positive to our farm. Birds certainly wouldn't require a costly high security containment system. In a weak moment on a dreary cloudy day, I waved the white flag.

Our small shed over the well pit was a perfect size for a small coop. It just needed some nesting boxes and a few minor repairs. Alex and I picked out a construction plan from one of our resource books and began assembling wood from the scrap piles in the barn. Randy helped us replace a broken window on the west side. Then we screwed plywood over the old cement pits that used to house the milk tanks. We built a nesting box with four stalls and repurposed old metal pipes into roosting bars.

One cold evening, Alex, Amie, Hannah, and I sat huddled under blankets on the couch perusing poultry catalogs. The wind howled around the house, rattling the living room windows. Jake and Ellie curled up on rugs nearby. Clyde rested his wide muzzle on the window ledge, watching snow fall. Faced with choices of hens versus roosters and numerous breeds, I quickly set limits on how many each child was allowed before we ended up with fifty fowl. Then I picked out twelve ducklings for myself. We placed our order the next day. The kids marked days off the calendar excitedly. The rest of February crawled by; there were very few mornings when the mercury crawled above frigid. Then, before I nearly lost my mind from cabin fever, rays of sunshine burst through the grey sky canopy. Strips of black earth appeared between snow drifts, and Blaze started to shed his shaggy winter coat. One early March morning, we received a frantic call from the postmaster imploring us to pick up our package. Loud chirping echoed in the background.

I drove into town after herding my protesting kids onto the bus. The postmaster quickly placed the box in my arms and ushered me outside. At home, I wrestled the noisy container out of the back seat and down the cellar door stairs. The basement was a temporary home for our new additions until it warmed up enough to transfer them to the coop. A warming lamp above a plastic pool containing straw, feeders, and a water dispenser awaited. There were two fatalities from the shipping in huge box riddled with air holes. I set their lifeless bodies aside for a proper burial service later. According to the several chicken guidebooks, the chicks needed to be taught where their food and water was. I picked up each tiny bird and dipped their beaks in the water before placing them next to the metal chick feed container. Their downy feathers were marvelously soft.

If one chick chirped, they all joined in. The noise level was surprisingly high, and they were quite lively for such a young age. They basked beneath the heat lamp in a lump of yellow feathers when they weren't eating and pooping. My ducks, evident by their rounded beaks and webbed feet, ate side by side with the chicks and tried to fit into the waterer. I monitored all of them for signs of disease and kept the food dishes full. When the bus dropped Alex, Amie, and Hannah off at the end of our lane, they raced inside, threw their backpacks, boots, and coats on the floor, and ran downstairs. Hannah tried to smuggle a duck beneath her sweatshirt to sleep with; I knew then that keeping the house clean was going to be even more challenging.

Within a few days each chick had a name. I couldn't keep them all straight. The bedding had to be changed daily, but my kids didn't complain. Instead, they happily divided up the chores. Alex and Amie dragged bags of filthy straw out the cellar doors and spread it in the compost pile. Hannah made sure there was always clean water and feed. They spent hours picking them up and playing with them in the cold basement. Those babies grew at an alarming rate; within a week we had erected higher walls around the pool. Despite with reinforcements, they still escaped almost daily.

Spring's arrival was heralded by cold winds and rain. Even at that early stage, chicken personalities were evident. Some were feisty while others were calm. The ammonia odor wafting up from the basement into the house grew stronger with each passing day. In early April, we decided it was finally warm enough to move our flock to their permanent home in the chicken shed.

That Sunday, Alex, Amie, and Hannah caught each fledgling, paraded them up the cellar steps, and deposited them in the coop's thick straw. Some scratched in the straw, some explored, and others just bellied up to the feeder. They seemed very happy to be free from the confines of the small plastic pool. Several took short flights from one end of the building to the other and crashed into the walls-- without any adverse effects thankfully. My ducks gravitated toward the large water bucket, splashing and sputtering. Chores were scheduled to be done twice daily, and I reminded the kids to shut the outside door tightly. I didn't want marauding raccoons to nab a tender chicken or duck dinner.

The chicks grew into the "ugly" adolescent stage: gangly, beaky things with adult feathers sprouting in random places. Their scaly legs were dinosaur-like, and combs with wattles appeared on the already aggressive roosters. The waddling and quacking ducks remained adorable throughout their metamorphosis but created muddy havoc everywhere. The kids patiently instructed me on each chicken's name, ensuring that all would live a long life. Pearl and Rusty were white leghorns, Feather and Crazy Jo were speckled brown hens, and Funk was our most colorful rooster with blue-green tail feathers.

Within several months our brood completed their transformation into mature chickens and ducks, with full feathers and yellow-orange eyes. As they grew, we realized our fowl needed an outdoor space. Once the soil dried out enough to work, Alex and I fenced in a small run along the western wall of the shed. The holes for the posts were much easier to dig than the ones for the picket fence had been. There were no trees in the immediate vicinity. Randy had taught me well. We hit some gravel but managed to work through that easily. After the posts were set, we stapled a heavy gauge wire fence along the length of the enclosure, along with a gate we could enter through. Then I dragged the plastic pool from the basement, put it in a corner of the pen, and filled it with water for the ducks.

We cut a small door in the western wall that we could open for our fowl in the morning and latch shut at night. A ramp with small blocks of wood to help them climb up and down was the final piece. The next day I stood by the ramp to help any that required assistance as Amie and Hannah shooed the chickens and ducks into the great outdoors. The birds were hesitant at first, until they discovered insects and little grass sprouts at the end of the ramp just waiting to be eaten.

As dusk neared, I returned to the shed for a flock check. All were roosting peacefully inside except for one lone duck. He could not figure out how to get back up the ramp. I chased him around the pen a few times until he was cornered, then grabbed him and popped him inside with the others. Latching the small door shut, I returned to the inside and replenished their food and water under the watchful eyes of the baby roosters. They glared haughtily down at me from their perches. After I closed the main door, I stood for a moment to admire the soft purple, orange, and pinks on the western horizon. A gurgle that might have been a crow floated away into the night air. I grinned. Welcoming chickens and ducks onto our farm had been a great decision. Life was good.

Chapter 32

ONCE OUR CASH FLOW IMPROVED with regular pharmacy paychecks, I began squirreling away small amounts of money for a second equine companion. Blaze deserved some time off, and I yearned for longer rides. My quarter horse was a wonderful mount, but his soft hooves did not tolerate gravel roads well. So, while my three did their homework on the dining room table, I perused local newspapers for candidates. The kids and I made several trips to meet prospects. A sorrel mare was sweet tempered, but her bone-jarring trot left me with a two-day headache. One spirited bay Arabian gelding took off so fast in his canter that I was almost ejected from the saddle. None of them possessed the endearing personality traits of my Blaze.

One sunny spring Saturday as I yanked crab grass from the raspberries, Amie tottered out to the garden in a pink bridesmaid dress and heels to tell me I had a call. She and Hannah were playing dress up. Brushing dirt off my hands, I followed her back to the house and sat down on the front porch with our portable phone. Clyde lay near the porch swing where Alex was engineering several vehicles from connectable plastic blocks and Hannah struggled with an old purple formal on the steps.

Amie helped her into it while I placed the receiver between my ear and shoulder and tied the back sashes on both their dresses. The call was from a friend of a friend who heard through the grapevine I was looking for a good horse. She was looking to downsize her herd because there just wasn't enough time to exercise all of them.

The following weekend I drove to her farm. After I unloaded my saddle, the owner's husband introduced me to Red, a rangy, crimson Tennessee Walker. His wife was at a seminar, so he saddled his thoroughbred mare while I cinched my saddle on Red. It was love at first ride. I adored the walker's long and powerful stride as we roamed the ditches and fields. When I coaxed him into a canter, his gait was as smooth as a rocking chair. Red was fast; at full gallop the ground blurred beneath us. I was grinning widely as I wrote a check for him before driving back to the farm.

Red calmly backed out of his trailer at our farm several weeks later and walked into the small pen like he owned the place. The spirited gelding assumed the role of alpha, bossing Blaze around with a toss of his head and nip of his teeth. My stocky palomino did not protest. He loved being a part of a herd again and meekly followed Red's leadership. Our new resident was very addicted to butterscotch treats and practically put his halter on himself to receive them. We were quickly running out of riding time as winter approached, but whenever I had a few free hours, I threw my saddle on Red. His tireless legs whisked me away from my cares and troubles.

Despite many efforts, I remained the lone horse lover of my family. Amie was bitten by the bug for a brief period, and we spent memorable afternoons laughing together as we rode our horses around the neighbors' fields. I loved watching her bounce in the saddle on Blaze's broad back. But then, just as quickly as she developed interest, it disappeared. Alex rode a few times before he decided snowboarding was his true passion, and Hannah stoutly refused to go near the stirrups.

The following summer, a friend introduced me to a new neighbor who lived just a few miles away. Her children participated in various fairs and horse exhibitions throughout the Midwest with their Ponies of America herd. Pat and I decided that once our kids faced blackboards and teachers in the fall, we would start riding together. Eagerly I waited for the rumbling yellow bus to pick up my three. I waved goodbye to them from the end of our lane, reining in my impulse to skip back to the house until they disappeared over the hill.

Pat rode in the direction of our farm after finishing her chores, and I guided Red up the road. We met halfway. After some nickering, prancing, and a nip or two, our horses seemed to get along. We pointed them up the nearby fire lane for a short introductory jaunt. Cammie kept up with Red's long strides with a smooth trot. After our first encounter, Pat and I grabbed every opportunity to ride together.

A nearby farm had been transformed into a wildlife sanctuary, and their trails quickly became our favorite escape. Tall prairie grasses and flowers covered gentle hills, and several dry creek beds meandered through thick green woods. We wound our way through the fields, into the maple forest, and jumped our horses over fallen trees where they blocked the path. One day we discovered a small wooden bridge. It took a few skirmishes as both horses took turns backing up, pinning their ears, and spinning around like rodeo ponies to get them over it. Red gave up first and clattered across. Cammie cautiously followed, unconvinced that horse-eating trolls didn't live beneath the bridge.

One mid-October day we loaded the horses into Pat's trailer and transported them to a local state park. Red and Cammie were bubbling with energy, dancing around while we girthed their saddles. We had plenty of miles to let them run. We cantered through tall pine groves, walking up steep rocky hills, and trotted along wide paths in the meadows. I was not sure how Red would tolerate his first creek crossing, but he waded right into the cold water and took a long drink. I sighed with relief; no contest of wills for a change. But as soon as I uttered that sigh, my horse circled in the middle of the stream, buckled at the knees, and plopped down in the cold water with me still straddling him.

Pat giggled, and I did too after I kicked my horse back onto to his feet. Then he gave a mighty shake which almost dislodged me. We were both soaked, but luckily the sun was warm. When we reached the end of a beautiful maple forest, where yellow and orange leaves fell softly to the ground, we decided it was time to return to the trailer. The horses could have gone longer, but their riders were tired and sore.

As soon as we entered the parking area, Asian beetles swarmed us. It was like being in a horror movie. Red bucked and reared; I guided him to the shade and dismounted before I was thrown. After yanking off their saddles, we trotted the horses into the trailer and slammed the door behind them. Retrieving our gear, we threw everything inside the truck and dove into the seats, smacking the bugs that landed on us. Further expeditions were postponed until the first frost killed off the insects.

Red became my go-to horse whenever I needed a quick exit from life's highway. He was never lame and always ready to run. My sweet quarter horse began to spend lots of time alone in the pasture. Pangs of guilt stabbed me every time I left Blaze's saddle on the hanger, even though he was probably relieved to have time off. One afternoon, Red and I met a different neighbor who was taking her new mare out for a trot. As our horses paced side by side, she told me that she had really enjoyed riding her old horse bareback but was not sure her new mount could be trusted. Riding Red without stirrups would be a certain invitation for a full body cast, but what about Blaze?

One sunny June afternoon, I caught and groomed both horses at their customary spots in the shed. After replacing Blaze's halter with a bridle, I led him outside. Red protested loudly and pawed anxiously at the ground.

Once Blaze was secured to a post, I returned to Red and turned him loose before he gave himself a heart attack. He wheeled and ran outside to discover his buddy standing on the opposite side of the long metal gate. Red shook his head and paced back and forth as I jumped the fence and prepared to mount my docile palomino.

I rolled a stout tree log over for use as a mounting block. Blaze snorted at it and danced around until I scratched his belly for a bit. We walked past it several times until he ignored it. Then I positioned him just right, stepped up onto the stump, swung my leg over his back, and vaulted up. Blaze eyed me in surprise. Breathing deeply to relax, I wiggled my sitting bones around until I felt balanced. With the reins in one hand and a fistful of mane in the other, I gently nudged him into a walk.

There was a spring to Blaze's step as we strolled around the yard. His ears swiveled back and forth, listening to my voice. It was easier to move to his gait without the heavy stiff saddle between us. Emboldened that I had not fallen yet, I steered Blaze toward the creek. We waded through tall grass that rippled like a green ocean around us and along the path near the tangled red twig dogwoods. Sparrows and robins sang to us from above. The young trees in our forest were finally thriving after all my hard work. Nests perched precariously on several branches we passed; I even spotted a few speckled eggs in one. Loosening my white-knuckled grip on Blaze's mane, I urged him into a slow trot. It felt like we were flying.

After our inaugural bareback experience, I hopped on Blaze whenever I did not want to wrestle with a saddle or Red's strong will. We leisurely toured our neighbors' farms and wandered along the grassy strips bordering the crop fields. I even gained enough confidence to coax him into a canter on the trails I'd mown through our fledgling forest. Bareback riding improved my abilities and balance immensely, even though my blue jeans ended up just as fuzzy as him.

As Pat and I continued our rides together through the seasons, we shared concerns about raising kids, managing our farms, and living our lives well. Whether I chose to wrestle Red or relax bareback on Blaze, those adventures became treasured memories. Parenthood worries and farmstead woes just seemed smaller on the backs of our horses. The beautiful countryside, set to the rhythm of hoof beats drumming the ground, buoyed us through all country challenges.

My geldings paid me back many times above their costs with their devoted companionship. Oats were about one hundred dollars a year, veterinarian expenses might run up to two hundred fifty, but a velvety nuzzle on my neck from one of my boys was priceless. For me, there was no place better than on the back of a horse I loved-- except perhaps our front porch swing with my three children cuddled around me.

Chapter 33

THE PANIC IN OUR NEIGHBOR'S VOICE over the phone one November evening sent the kids and I running to the van, pulling on coats and boots. Several of their valuable beef calves were missing, it was dark, and the coyotes were yipping. The kids and I bumped up their lane, met the neighbors outside their barn, and devised a quick plan for the round-up. We headed to the recently harvested corn field where we found a break in the barbed wire fence. After carefully stepping over it, we stumbled through the stubble until our flashlights illuminated the bovines munching stray corn cobs. We spread out and slowly guided them back through the broken fence and into a small pen without losing anyone to the coyotes (kids included). The neighbor thanked us profusely as we drove away. Despite the adrenaline flowing from our late-night quest, Alex, Amie and Hannah dove under their covers as soon as we got home. I was exhausted, but too wired to sleep.

Our farm was still my sanctuary, despite never-ending battles of chopping thistles, bathing dogs that insisted on rolling on decomposed varmints, and nagging the kids to clean the chicken coop. I loved living in the country with all its misadventures. And visualizing the panorama from my front porch swing gave me strength to smile through angry customers' tirades about the high cost of medications or long wait times. But when all my burdens became so overwhelming that even a flight on Blaze or Red ceased to comfort me, a girlfriend retreat was the medicine I needed.

Long before babies bounded into our lives, my high school friend Julie and I had booked a getaway for the two of us. She was dealing with a full-time job and young children, I with seventy hours of research projects and two destructive canines. She found a spa nestled on an old farmstead with 50 acres of land and a pond that advertised fitness classes, walking paths, and an indoor pool. It even included self-help classes guaranteed to transform us from frazzled to confident.

It was late spring, but there were still small patches of lingering snow remaining from the last storm. After a two-hour drive, we pulled into a lane lined with massive oaks; I caught a glimpse of inviting wooded trails and a pond. We checked in and were guided to our stark room which felt a little like a college dormitory. Once our duffel bags were unpacked, we wandered into the dining room to join other guests at a table for lunch-- a vegetarian lunch. Even though I had become fairly health conscious, I wasn't quite ready to give up meat. But their veggie lasagna was excellent, and the salads were very fresh. Sadly, there was no dessert on the menu. My sweet tooth walked away from the table grateful for the bag of snacks I'd concealed inside my duffel as emergency supplies. Julie and I returned to our room and feasted on smuggled chocolate chip cookies and greasy potato chips as we talked late into the night.

The next morning, we ate our meatless breakfast without protest and reported for fitness classes. I was not overly fond of the t-shirt and shorts provided; they reminded me of the hideous one-piece baby blue striped high school gym outfit that still gave me nightmares. I opted for a step aerobics class but caught the instructor worriedly watching me as I stumbled through the session. Peaceful laps in the pool were better.

And once I was walking the hiking trails, I was happy. That night, over fresh bread and minestrone soup sans sausage, we discussed our day. I was exhausted from all the fresh air, information from self-improvement classes, and exercise. When my head hit the hard pillow, I immediately fell into a dreamless slumber.

The small relaxation area did not offer much in the way of atmosphere, but we enjoyed our final day despite its lack of privacy. I had never had a facial or massage before and felt incredibly pampered afterwards. After a final luncheon, we bid our spa mates goodbye and climbed into our car to head home. We also stopped at the first convenience store we spotted on the highway. Laughing as I greedily tore open a cupcake wrapper, I thanked Julie for planning our trip.

That weekend away had been an extremely worthwhile investment. We decided to make it an annual event. Future adventures would revolve around gourmet food, chocolate, wine, and a new resort that offered a huge swimming pool, modern fitness classes, wonderful restaurants, and a bar. We invited more friends and my sister-in-law Bev to join us. There were no generic shorts and shirts awaiting us on stiff single beds; instead, the comfortably appointed rooms had two queen beds, a fireplace, and a patio. We wore our own clothes to work out in and dressed up for gourmet dinners.

During the day we pursued different activities. Julie discovered a water aerobics class taught by an exotic Italian instructor and happily ran lengths of the pool at his direction. I sweated to the pounding beat of a stationary group bicycle workout that threatened to kill me. We both giggled our way through several yoga classes, feeling like doughy pretzels twisting into shapes.

One year I ventured out on a trail ride instead of grinding through a bike class. "Mr. Cowboy," dressed in a long leather duster jacket that swung with his movements, saddled up two horses. I was the only guest that braved a ride after a winter storm swept through the area. We raced our horses in six inches of powdery snow through the woods. I hung on to the saddle horn for dear life while dodging branches and tree trunks. I didn't mind being whipped in the face by my horse's mane; it was one of the most memorable rides I'd ever had. "Mr. Cowboy," like Julie's water aerobics instructor, was handsome and fun. He occasionally made guest appearances in my dreams.

Sometimes Julie and I skipped yoga class and drove to the quaint downtown area to wander shops filled with expensive clothes and shoes. Before dinner, we lounged in over-stuffed lobby chairs sipping Chardonnay and listening to the relaxing sounds of a pianist playing a baby grand piano. Our meals were amazing, especially since we didn't have to cook or do the dishes. Then we shimmied to live music at the disco until the early morning hours.

It was on one of those girlfriend weekends that I re-discovered the joy of pretty shoes. Opportunities to dress up in the country were rare, especially with footwear. All my high heels from corporate life had been donated to charity before we moved to the farm; they were hardly functional in muck and mud. Even at the pharmacy, my footwear had to be comfortable enough to stand for long shifts.

Julie and I chatted during the drive to Indianapolis this time as I jotted down notes for a romance novel we were going to write together. Our inspiration had appeared at a small-town gas station in the form of one shirtless, deeply tanned young man who had pulled up to the pumps on the other side. Muscles rippled along his bare back as he cleaned the windows of his rusty pick-up truck. I fanned myself with a magazine and swooned when Julie caught my eye. The miles passed quickly. After arriving at our friend's house, we enjoyed a child-free dinner and crashed into her guest beds.

I had recently taken up jogging to regain some of my elusive pre-pregnancy fitness. The next morning, while both my friends slept in, I ran out the front door-- and promptly got lost on the winding subdivision streets. When I finally found my way back, I was amazed to discover them still lingering over coffee instead of hitting the mall early. They waited while I took a quick shower and wolfed down some donuts. The mall was swarming with shoppers on that beautiful fall day; I was glad I'd run first. We circled the parking lot for fifteen minutes before a spot opened a half mile away from the entrance.

    I mumbled something about finding a quiet corner to write in, but my friends demanded that I accompany them while they browsed. Our first stop was a large department store, complete with its own shoe wing. Julie was a self-acknowledged shoe-a-holic and, having failed a twelve-step recovery program multiple times, quickly disappeared into the clearance area. My other friend followed. Feeling a little lost, I wandered around the store, dodging sales ladies loaded with perfume bottles misting everyone within reach and cosmetic consultants beckoning me with little vials of makeup. I escaped that area and idly poked through some clothing, but it was hard to imagine wearing anything from those racks while I shoveled manure. Bored, I walked back to my friends who were hidden behind a small mountain of shoe boxes. I sighed, found my size, and plopped down on a bench to see what the fuss was about.

    Wrestling off my rank tennis shoes, I furtively looked around to make sure nearby noses didn't wrinkle in disgust. No other customers retched in the immediate vicinity, so I strapped on some black high heels and carefully stood up. I tentatively placed my right foot in front of the left. Wobbled. Grabbed the shelf for support. Then I put my left foot before my right foot. Swayed for a moment. Then repeated. After a few minutes, I let go of the shelves and found my stride. It was fun. Rubber barn boots certainly did not make my hips sway like those shoes did. My friends clapped when they saw me sashaying about. I tried a runway spin, stumbled, and landed unceremoniously on the same bench I started out on, laughing with them.

My toes screamed in protest at their tight confinement. But the shoes made me feel a lot more girl than farm, which was nice for a change. Pulling random boxes off the racks, I tried at least twenty different styles until I settled on a pretty pair with moderate heels that fit my budget. A pink bag filled with new panties soon accompanied the box of shoes. We had been wandering the mall for several hours; I begged for a break. My friends finally allowed me to take shelter in a coffee shop while they finished perusing the remaining shops. I jotted ideas down in my always-present notebook and sipped a latte for an hour until they collected me. Then we wedged our packages into the car's trunk and headed home.

Later that night (after a nap), the three of us dined alfresco at an elegant Italian bistro. As we strolled the trendy revitalized area, my friends encouraged me to walk ahead of them so they could watch the reactions in my wake. They observed that the male of our species liked high heels too, because I turned a few heads. Back at the house, all three of us nodded off in the middle of a romantic comedy. When Julie and I waved farewell to our friend and pointed the car home the next morning, my feet throbbed but my spirits (and wallet) were lighter.

I happily threw myself back into the whirlwind of work, animal husbandry, and family after we arrived home. Every time I pulled on chore boots, I paused to admire those pretty heels in my basket. I couldn't bear to let them get stained with green chicken manure, so they were relocated to my closet. Occasionally I wore them to work, where they magically enabled me to serenely listen to irritated customers, doctors, and nurses. Their secret powers rivaled my cute panties in guiding me through busy rural days.

After a year, I decided it was time to bequeath the sling-backs to Amie. I kept finding them in her room anyway; they worked better than muck boots for fashion shows. Eventually Hannah pirated those heels from her, which started a never-ending war involving stealthy missions at midnight searching under beds for the booty. I finally gave in and took both girls shopping to purchase new pairs of heels for all of us. But the smuggling never stopped; shoes were always prettier in someone else's closet.

Life without girlfriend weekend retreats was unfathomable. The simple joys of dressing up, exercising to a good sweatiness, and buying an occasional pair of ridiculous shoes were treasured memories. But the highlight of those times was really the simple delight in spending time with my friends. Late night discussions and lively debates alternated with quiet moments of solitude. Laughter over shared tales of child rearing and tears over relationship struggles left us all with poignant moments. Those weekends provided a wonderful sense of renewal and buoyed me through life's challenges after I returned to the farm. I was thankful to have such wonderful soul mates to ponder life's mysteries with.

Chicken Strips

Chapter 34

A STRANGE BOOM PIERCED THE NIGHT, startling me from a bad dream featuring the well pit, a foot of water, and dangling extension cords. Even though the noise probably meant an emergency trip outside, I was grateful to have been woken up; the nightmare had been horrifying. My ears strained to listen for the sound again, but all was silent except for the cricket chorus drifting in through my window. I rolled over and willed my overactive imagination to dream a more pleasant scenario as I counted chickens in my head (they were more effective than sheep).

Our move to the country had relieved us of the noisy suburban rhythm of sirens, honking horns, and all the other sounds associated with dense populations. But there was no such thing as absolute silence, even in remote rural areas. Deep tractor growls and ghostly animal howls echoed eerily through the hills instead.

After mentally counting eleven hens, two sounds disrupted my count. This time a shriek followed the loud bang. Was one of our female cats inviting every male within a six-mile range over for a tryst? Or a coyote mom calling her pups to a fresh kill? Maybe Clyde had cornered a raccoon in the barn again (it rarely ended well for the masked interloper). And none of those scenarios explained what was making that banging noise. I grumbled and shuffled from my bedroom, grabbed a robe off the hook and pulled on my boots in the mudroom. Clyde met me at the back door. There was no battle evidence on his sweet face, so I did a cursory check in all the buildings. He followed me as I counted beaks and noses.

BOOM! Clyde and I both jumped. BOOM! The sound was coming from the machine shed. After we skirted around our bonfire ring, I pulled one of the huge sliding doors open and hit the light switch. Dim light illuminated stacks of round hay bales which our neighbor stored there. Then I spotted the culprit. The twelve-foot-high aluminum sliding door at the east end was hanging from only one roller on the track; when the wind puffed, the heavy door swung wider and slammed against its frame. Metal on metal accounted for the shriek.

A long wooden step ladder hung behind the Ford tractor. I unhooked it, carried it to the opening, and propped it against the wall. Then I went outside and pushed the heavy door closed, trying not to think about what would happen if it crashed down on top of me. Panic-fueled adrenaline gave me the strength to move the awkward panel into place. Then I wedged pieces of broken cement against the steel bottom to keep it snug against the frame.

Moving quickly, I returned to the inside of the shed. The cement wasn't going to keep the door from blowing open for long. It seemed the best temporary solution was to wire the door to the frame. rummaged through tools on the bench and found heavy wire, cutters, nails, and a hammer. Dragging the supplies up the ladder I placed beside the frame, I pounded nails at intervals into the wood. Then I threaded wire around each of the two by four braces on the inner part of the door and looped it back around the nail, twisting the ends together tightly and banging the nail backwards to secure it. After the last set was finished, I climbed down and gently pushed against the huge slider. It held.

I threw my tools back on the bench and left the ladder where it was. Clyde walked with me back to the house, then trotted to his station on the front porch. Just as I pulled off my boots on the mud porch, Ellie almost knocked me over with her enthusiastic greeting and a bonus spaghetti noodle dangling from her mouth. She and Jake had gotten into the trash again. I disregarded the little voice that nudged me to clean up the mess and simply collapsed into bed instead like my single carefree-career-self recommended. I listened for a few minutes but only heard the soft hooting of an owl outside my window.

Our family contributed to the country noises too. Screams from Amie and Hannah had me leaping down the porch steps in my robe the next morning, cup of coffee in hand. Jake and Ellie sat proudly next to a possum lying in our lane. I had not even known they escaped. There were no signs of life when I cautiously prodded the still form with my slipper. Herding the kids to the end of the driveway where the bus awaited, I waved to the driver. Then I trudged back into the house, changed out of my pajamas, and coaxed the dogs inside with treats. An early morning burial was not how I envisioned spending my free morning. I stomped to the garden shed and dug through all the tools until I found our shovel. But when I walked back out to the yard with it, my victim was nowhere in sight! The critter had truly "played possum."

Later that same day, I heard a very loud yelp from Clyde. Skunks were unusual on our farm, but occasionally one strayed onto our land. The odor from a direct hit was not the same skunky scent that permeated roadkill. It was worse. Clyde and I shivered through multiple tomato juice applications that day, both red from head to toe. The net result of those treatments was a dog that smelled like a well-seasoned Italian skunk. He spent the rest of that week in his cozy doghouse until I found a product that contained enzymes and essential oils. After several baths with that, he was finally allowed back into the house where he left a fresh minty scent in his wake.

While reading the Sunday paper one weekend, "moos" closer than usual drifted in through the window. Glancing outside, I spied a heifer cavorting in our front yard. As I raced out the door, a small herd of them trotted by with fragile tomato plants dangling from their lips. They ran down the road toward home, but their party in my garden was evidenced by trampled young seedlings. Devastated, I wandered from plant to plant, gently replacing the uprooted ones back into the ground and patting loose dirt around the remaining wobbly stems for support. Amazingly enough, so many plants survived and flourished that by harvest time I wished the young cows had eaten more.

Was it a tragedy that our home in the middle of nowhere lacked total peace and quiet? I did not think so. Rural noises taught me to appreciate rare moments of silence, like when snow fell thickly on a winter morning and muffled every sound. I treasured quiet times on the porch steps watching the sun color the east with red and yellow while I sipped a warm cup of coffee. Sure, I lost more than a little sleep to wild things and buildings intent on self-destruction. But patrolling our grounds in the wee hours gave me a rare chance to view the dark heavens. Thousands of stars winked down at me as if they were just as amused by my country adventures as I was.

Chapter 35

HANNAH AND I LOUNGED IN THE HAMMOCK with Feather and Rusty in our laps. Pleasant warmth radiated from the chickens as they lay quietly. Amie, sitting between us, read aloud from a book. Alex rode up and down the lane on a rusty but functional banana seat bicycle. Stacks of homework sat on the dining room table, but the day was too gorgeous to be cooped up inside.

The chickens had endeared themselves to us. Hannah was especially enchanted with them. I reminded her constantly that hens and roosters were not house pets every time she smuggled one in beneath a towel to sit with her on the couch. She was usually involved in some kind of "fowl" play when not in school.

Bird behavior was a fascinating study. The hens were mild-mannered once the pecking order was established, but the roosters transformed into leaders. A special cluck from the males signaled there was food nearby, and hens came running. A brilliant Rhode Island Red rooster we named Funk was the chief; our sassy White Leg Horn Rusty was his second lieutenant. Both bossed their female counterparts around by snaking their long necks to the ground, lifting one wing, and pacing menacingly until the hens followed their lead. Like most farm kids, mine learned about the birds and the bees at a young age.

Chicken-related vocabulary words sprinkled our conversations. "Hennish" described someone who was being protective or motherly. "Puffed" referred to the roosters when they inflated their chests and shook out their feathers. "One eye" was the rooster attack look when they turned their head to focus on the intended victim and began a side-stepping advance. "Fluffed" meant that your stomach was full and you were happy. I had to mind my words when counseling pharmacy patients, so I didn't slip into "chicken speak."

Our flock pecked their outdoor pen clean in a month, we opened the gate and allowed them to wander the yard in search of bugs and tender sprouts. The freedom gave them exercise and extra nutrients. I was worried for the first few evenings, until every bird instinctively returned to the coop at dusk just like our chicken references said they would. The only problem with our flock was that they did not understand road etiquette. They strolled across the gravel to the neighbor's corn field whenever they felt like it; the worms were fatter over there. Luckily, we didn't have much traffic. And I gained excellent sprinting and dodging practice chasing them back to our yard with a broom.

Our roosters were extremely territorial and protected their harem from all perceived intruders, including us. Since their brains were the size of a pea, they didn't realize we were the ones who fed them. Often I was in the middle of weeding one of the flower gardens, stood to stretch my back, and discovered rooster spurs (the dagger-like nails on the back of their feet) aimed at my calves. Hannah entertained herself by capturing hens and making them squawk so a rooster would dash to their aid. Then she laughingly sprinted away with Rusty or Funk hot at her heels.

Visitors to the farm didn't always fare well. Several of my friends were chasing victims and suffered from chicken-induced PTSD. On one occasion, a friend offered to feed the horses while we spent the day in Chicago, a summer outing that became an annual tradition. As she threw Blaze and Red hay and checked their water, she heard a rustling behind her. When she turned around, Rusty was giving her the one-eye. She laughed until he began edging toward her. Backing into a corner, she stumbled over a rake (luckily the kids never put anything away) and used it to fend him off. The same thing happened to Julie one day when she dropped off beef that we had purchased together. She carried the first load into the house and was on her way out for the second when Funk chased her onto the tailgate of her vehicle. She brandished an umbrella to keep him at bay while delivering the rest of the meat. After those incidents, we always instructed visitors on rooster defense and provided stout sticks.

Chickens and ducks left their pungent ammonia signatures everywhere. It fertilized weeds in the yard and provided filler for the open grooves on our tennis shoes and my car tires. That distinctive country aroma followed us wherever we traveled so we never felt far from home. Cleaning the yard was futile; it was enough to clean up after our canines. At least chicken chores were not as labor intensive as goat work had been. It still wasn't fun. Alex, Amie, and Hannah spent more time searching for scrapers and shovels. After watching them half-heartedly move straw around, I'd just take over. Physical farm labor was a welcome change from the pharmacy's mental challenges anyway. But a clean coop was just like a clean house: satisfying, but seldom long-lived.

Hannah ran into the kitchen one day, cradling the first precious egg in her hands. Alex and Amie cheered; I'm pretty sure they saw dollar signs printed on it. I quietly returned to mixing batter for a coffee cake while they plotted how to spend their soon-to-be-had fortune. The treasure hunt began. Every day the kids excitedly gathered the eggs in an old Easter basket we repurposed from the attic. Each chicken breed laid different colors; there were white ones, blue ones, light green ones, and of course brown ones. Every oval was perfectly smooth, sometimes still warm and had yolks that were bright orange instead of the limpid yellow store-bought variety.

Egg money was deposited into a jar on the kitchen counter. It provided a little spending money for the Saturday farmers' market on Madison's downtown square. On one of those trips, Alex discovered a booth where a woman sewed tiny stuffed roosters from glittery material. We purchased three that morning. Soon our flock of stuffed roosters approached the number of real chickens. On rainy days, Alex, Amie, and Hannah built rooster villages with the old building block sets and plastic cars they dragged down from the attic.

Eventually each child adopted a favorite real chicken. Feather was our tamest hen and sported brown feathers speckled with black and tiny bits of down under her beak like a beard. Alex taught her how to skateboard, pushing her gently along the barn floor as Feather's scaly claws gripped the edges tightly. She rode shotgun in the beat-up battery-operated plastic jeep I had purchased at a garage sale. His driving skills improved greatly as they motored slowly around the yard; he didn't want to crash with her in the passenger seat.

Amie took her hen Bubba sledding on the barn hill and read her stories in the hammock. The quiet little hen even napped beside her on the porch swing. Bubba did not mind being dressed up in an old toddler outfit and sat quietly in an umbrella stroller while Amie pushed her up and down the lane, avoiding Alex and Feather in the jeep.

Hannah's favorite chicken was Rusty. His crows filled the house whenever she smuggled him inside to watch television and made me smile even as I chopped onions. The rooster's talons usually sported hot pink or bright purple nail polish thanks to her efforts. I believe the other roosters made fun of him. That rooster chased Hannah as much as she chased him. He was most likely the reason she would excel at cross country running in her high school years.

It became a tradition to bring one of our chickens inside as a surprise guest during our gatherings and holiday open houses. Many of our friends had never been up close and personal to a live chicken. Their fowl interactions had been via Styrofoam and plastic packaging in grocery stores. We invited them to touch a rooster wattle or hen comb while we held the chickens; the bright red appendages were firm and spongy. And of course, their feathers were very soft. But when the hen or rooster started to reach for the cheese platters on the counter or decorated Christmas cookies, they were whisked back to the coop.

Our fowl provided entertainment with their silly antics and gave us plenty of exercise. Ducks reminded us of the joy of splashing in puddles. All their endearing personalities guaranteed them absolute amnesty from my stew pot. Every time I observed someone warming their feathers in the sunshine or luxuriating in a dust bath, I was reminded to relax myself. Life was too short to spend it constantly pecking away at responsibilities.

Janet's Chicken Nuggets and Mashed Potatoes

- chicken tenderloins, chunked
- mayonaise
- crushed butter crackers

Preheat oven to 350°. Coat chicken with mayonaise, then toss in cracker crumbs. Bake until tender.

- 3 medium gold potatoes
- 4 T. butter
- 4 ounces cream cheese

Cook peeled & cubed potatoes in boiling water til soft. Drain, mash, and whip with butter and cream cheese.

Chapter 36

THERE WERE NOT MANY MONEY-MAKING opportunities for young children in the country. The egg business had not expanded into the multi-million-dollar franchise Alex, Amie, and Hannah had envisioned. Occasionally I offered jobs for pay like digging weeds or cleaning the horse shed. There were seldom any takers. So, when the kids asked permission to set up a lemonade and egg stand one summer afternoon, I wholeheartedly approved.

As they gathered supplies, I sat on the front porch next to Clyde and leafed through my lawn mower manual. The ancient machine sat sullenly beneath the silver maple, waiting for me to fix whatever was making a horrible grinding noise. There had to be an explanation inside the tattered pages. I was tired of spending more time prodding and poking at its moving parts than cutting grass. Maybe my father was right, and it was time to invest in a new mower.

Not finding any easy explanations for the mower, I wandered inside the house and made sure the kids had clean utensils and pitchers. Then I quickly returned to the porch, so I did not witness powdered lemonade mix spilling onto my just-mopped kitchen floor. The screen door repeatedly banged open and shut as Alex dragged an old card table outside, followed by several folding chairs. Hannah and Amie hauled the pitcher of lemonade and red plastic cups to the table. Then the girls drew signs for the yard with construction paper next to me on the porch floor. I only had to help a little with the lettering.

Alex had placed the rickety table a mere six inches from the road's edge. It was a bit too close for my comfort. He rolled his eyes at my concerns and moved everything back a few feet. The girls taped one sign to the table. Then they plucked my pink plastic flamingos from their nesting spots in a flower bed, taped a sign to each, and positioned them strategically in the ditches. More items were paraded to the table, including beach towels, a portable music player, snacks, and Feather the hen.

For the first five minutes, the children got along. Hannah sat on a beach towel under the table with the chicken. Alex and Amie took turns playing songs on the boom box. Then a plume of dust appeared over the hill. The kids assumed spots by the stand, and our neighbor stopped his old pick-up truck at the edge of the road.

After he waved to me, he walked over to their stand, and purchased a cup of lemonade. That started an argument over who poured and who took the money. Surprisingly, the kids worked a solution among themselves. Our neighbor chatted for a few minutes, and then drove home with a dozen eggs as well. Amie jingled the coins in their coffee can. I strolled out to their stand with a camera hidden behind my back and snapped a few shots before they had a chance to duck.

A light breeze tossed several cups into the tall grass; Amie ran them down. Hannah caught Pearl after Feather escaped and was chased by Rusty through the front yard. Back in the swing, I closed my eyes and dozed a bit. The lonely road stretched before us. Alex brought some jars of salsa outside to sell at five dollars a jar, but only offered to pay me fifty cents for my labor. I told him to return them to the basement shelves (he had good entrepreneurial potential).

As the day wore on, attention spans waned. Thirsty travelers were scarce in our neighborhood. Fights ensued. A plate of warm cookies quelled one loud disagreement, so I decided to ignore the grinding noise and cut the grass while peace prevailed. As I chugged around the yard, Alex wandered to the nearby pine tree and immersed himself in a book. Hannah caught Rusty and painted his talons red. Amie read a magazine.

Suddenly the wind shifted. Thunderheads billowed across the southern sky. I quickly backed the mower into its corner of the machine shed and helped the kids gather their things as the stormfront raced toward us. As we settled on the swing, Alex counted out the money from their sales. The lemonade stand had netted exactly six dollars. He felt entitled to all of it; the idea had been his. Amie and Hannah each wanted a share because they had mixed the product and gathered the eggs. I laughed and told them their sales did not even cover the cost of raw materials. The debate dragged on as lightning streaked across the sky and thunder rumbled through the thick air. We watched from the porch swing and ate popcorn. After dividing the coins in their coffee can, each child received two dollars and a lesson in economics. And what did I receive? One of my favorite country memories.

Chapter 37

AN ANGRY CUSTOMER APPROACHED ME just as I swung the metal gate down. She demanded that her pain medication be filled right away. It was thirty minutes past closing time, and I had just dispensed eleven orders from a last-minute hospital release. A headache throbbed behind my eyes. Sighing, I pushed the gate back up, but accidentally touched the emergency button. A deafening siren sounded, and our store manager raced over. Before words could escape his red face, I awoke in a cold sweat. It was only a nightmare.

My steady income had rescued the farm from financial ruin, but the stress of working in a box store pharmacy was getting to me. Despite regular equine escapes and girlfriend weekends, I worried constantly about making mistakes, keeping up with the farm maintenance, and whether the kids were learning too much from other kids on the bus.

Salvation appeared one dreary, rainy April morning. It was my day off. Locked alone in the bathroom for a few precious minutes, I tried to block out the whines of three kids who were home sick with ear and sinus infections. As they pounded on the door and cried pitifully for another movie, a magazine article caught my eye. I sighed, scratched Ellie's head (she had escaped with me) and opened the door.

"Bored with your workout?" the page asked as I wrestled child number one off my arm and pried my legs away from child number two and three. "Train for a triathlon" it proclaimed, and I laughed out loud, finally giving in to the children's demands for attention. I put the magazine aside and herded them into the kitchen for snacks. After I dosed them with ibuprofen and antibiotics, they feverishly clustered around me on the couch as I hit the "play" button for one of their favorite movies.

Later that evening, I collapsed in a chair and idly flipped through the three television channels we received. That article came back to haunt me. I found it under a pile of doll clothes. Could a mom like me finish an event like that? Was it possible to swim four hundred meters, bike seventeen miles, and run three miles all in one day? Maybe it was time to reclaim my body; six solid years of incubating and lactating had done little for my waistline.

I mulled the idea over once the kids were back in school. Chopping thistles hadn't decreased my pant size or totally rid me of underarm jiggles. Whenever I forgot my chicken stick and had to sprint to the back door with Rusty in hot pursuit, I gasped for oxygen. My blood pressure edged toward the high side. It was time to do something about it. One Saturday, I announced to Alex, Amie and Hannah that I would compete in a triathlon. There were no cheers, just a muffled mixture of clucking and giggling coming from their living room blanket tent. After peeking around one of the couch cushions, I spotted Rusty, Bubba and Feather under the covers with the kids. I sent everyone, fowl and human, outside.

A sprint race seemed a reasonable goal for me. Three months was plenty of time to get into shape. I had recently joined a fitness club with a pool and shower facilities so I could work out before my pharmacy shifts. With a training schedule taped next to the kid's chore chart on the refrigerator, I dove into my new project.

Dismayed at how long one mile seemed on the stationary bike, I wondered if the odometer was wrong. No one around me was drenched in perspiration like I was. Reading a magazine for distraction didn't help; I was blinded by sweat. My legs screamed for mercy, so I crawled off the bike after two miles and limped to the locker room.

My next trip to the club called for a swim workout. After one lap, I clutched the cement edge and sucked air like a freshly landed tuna. The gentle introduction to running didn't fare much better. My knees and hips cracked horribly when I broke from a walk to slow jog on the indoor track. But my dismal initial performances didn't stop me from doggedly pursuing all three activities. I was committed to finishing the event. Soon I looked forward to the rhythmic strokes in the pool, the steady beat of my feet on the pavement, and the clicking gears on the stationary bicycle. My distances increased, and the body staring back at me in the mirror was firmer.

Race day dawned hot and humid. Nervous butterflies in my stomach discouraged any thought of breakfast. When I pulled into the parking lot for the event, I felt incredibly conspicuous-- and very in awe of the athletes around me. Volunteers guided me through the registration process, marking race numbers on our legs and arms with permanent black ink. I yelled at the kids for doing things like that. Alex, Amie, and Hannah arrived with Bev and watched as I found my place in line at the pool. Swimmers ahead of me darted through the water like seals. When it was my turn, I was too busy trying not to drown from all the splashing to care about my turtle-paced breaststroke. The kids held up signs to cheer me on. After my last lap, I climbed up the ladder, gave my children drippy hugs and sloshed outside.

Wrestling shorts over my wet swimsuit took precious minutes. Then I peddled the opposite direction until a course marshal corrected me. Finally on open roads, I began to relax. The seventeen-mile bike ride wound past pretty farms and fields. Frequent shouts of "on your left" alerted me to when I was being passed by other racers.

When I reached the halfway mark, the scenery became decidedly less interesting. Where was the rest area with snacks? I stopped under a tree to eat a granola bar and nodded to the passing cyclists who asked if I was alright. Continuing onward after stuffing the wrapper in my shorts, I gritted my teeth and forced my unwilling calves to pedal through the remaining miles. Back at the parking lot, I dismounted the bike and staggered off for a three-mile run.

As I embarked on the out and back running course, I noticed most competitors were already returning toward the finish line. There was only one runner ahead of me. Distracting myself by singing songs in between gasps for breath helped me wobble along. At the turn around, my brother had parked my van nearby. Hannah's worried gaze from the rear window encouraged me to stop plodding, wave cheerily, and smile (it was probably more of a grimace of pain, but hey I tried).

With a mile to go, I stopped under a mulberry tree and popped some ripe fruit into my mouth. Sensation slowly returned to my toes. I was tempted to sit for a minute but knew I would never get back up if I did. Wiping my hands on my shorts, I walked until the celebration tent was in sight. Somehow my wooden legs managed to propel me over the blessed yellow tape on the pavement and into the arms of my family.

I was last in finishing the race that day; an eighty-one-year-old had crossed the line two minutes before me. My free-spirit-career-self was not impressed. But I didn't care; regular work outs had given me more energy than I had felt in years. That unimpressive finish in the triathlon did not deter me from further fitness efforts. Cleaning the horse shed and refereeing Amie and Hannah as they fought over clothes was easier with my improved endurance. Rusty the rooster couldn't outsprint me anymore, but I realized running was not my thing. Swimming gave me chlorine headaches. How could I maintain my improved condition? It was a dilemma solved by a friend who recommended group cycling classes on stationary bicycles. But the only session that meshed with my pharmacy schedule was at five thirty in the morning. I despised my alarm already but decided try it.

The first time my shadow darkened the door to that room, there was only one bike unoccupied. It was a popular class. I threw a leg over the seat, placed my feet in the cages, and pedaled my way through the most intense physical challenge I had ever experienced. I thought my heart would explode right out of my chest.

The second time, I managed to cycle through forty-five minutes without feeling like I was looking Death in the face. Our instructor did his best to distract us from the pain in our lungs by telling hilarious tales during short breaks in the thumping music. My classmates secretly taught me how to fake adding tension while he wasn't looking. Soon I found myself waking up before my shrill alarm in anticipation of the sessions. That disheveled and perspiring group of people grew into a bunch of new friends.

Months passed into seasons. My improved fitness gave me more energy to play kickball with the kids and evade Funk while I gathered eggs. Items on "The Lists" were getting checked off more frequently. Even when I was bombarded by prescriptions at the pharmacy, I felt calm and capable. Proud of my body for the first time in years, I purchased new form-fitting clothes when they were on sale.

One morning our spin instructor announced that he and his wife were moving and needed someone to take his place. I couldn't imagine life without a daily dose of endorphins anymore. It was even more terrifying to imagine our group disbanded. When no one else stepped forward to lead, my hand went up. I attended a certification class in the Chicago suburbs and was further intimidated by the incredible athletes there. But the instructor told me to relax and just have fun.

After a few months of teaching, I found that I really enjoyed coordinating workouts to music and motivating my classmates. A year flew by. Then one morning a new person showed up. He put special pedals on his bike so he could wear his cycling shoes. The cleats protruded from the bottom of the soles and made him walk like a duck.

After several weeks, the new guy started to introduce us to the secret world of cycling. His love for the sport was evident as he spun story after story. He encouraged me to give outdoor cycling a try, but I had never been much of a competitor. He persisted and managed to cajole me into wearing spandex and a hand-me down pair of cycling sandals. Both made a tremendous difference in my comfort, even though the padded shorts made my butt look big. After much cajoling, he finally convinced me to go for a casual ride on the roads near his farm with his wife and one of her friends, both experienced athletes.

An entire flock of butterflies danced in my belly as I pulled my recent purchase, a second-hand steel bike, from the back of my truck. After the women turned my helmet around so I wasn't wearing it backwards, they tightened the straps on my pedals so my feet wouldn't fall out. I wasn't sure I liked the sensation of being trapped and wobbled at the start. But once I got the hang of it, I was able to keep up as we rolled along quiet rural roads. I admired how skillfully they pedaled, chatting and shifting easily at the same time. I was just happy to remain upright. It took months before I felt comfortable trusting those skinny tires on the hard pavement. But my love for cycling grew. I learned how to ride in a group and discovered a talent for climbing hills.

Cycling became a new passion for me, another avenue to revel in the peaceful country around me. Within my pedaling reach were vistas of Wisconsin farmland, tall ridges above picturesque valleys, quiet tree-lined Illinois country roads, steep climbs, and breathtaking back-road descents. Red-tailed hawks screeched their calls in the early mornings above me, and Holsteins raced ahead along fence lines. As I grew stronger, my bike gave me a renewed sense of who I was and provided welcome stress relief. The joy of riding those skinny wheels introduced me to the hidden athlete inside I never knew existed.

Terry's Party Mints

16 ounces powdered sugar

8 ounces cream cheese

Mint flavor

regular sugar

Dust candy molds with regular sugar. Soften cream cheese, add powdered sugar, flavoring, and food color if desired. Press mix into molds, then pop out and let sit on wax paper for a bit. Store in air tight containers.

Chapter 38

IT WAS A BEAUTIFUL SEPTEMBER AFTERNOON, so I caught Blaze and rode him bareback down to the creek instead of facing the hundreds of ripening tomatoes on the dining room table. My legs were stronger with all the bike riding I'd done that summer, which had greatly improved my riding ability. Blaze sedately ambled around our burn pile of broken branches, tree trimmings, and weeds behind the barn. Riding him was a pleasant change from Red, who fought mightily when asked to walk by that area; he was convinced that a mountain lion liked to linger there and spooked every time. Blaze knew better. I noted some of the high tensile wires required tightening again as we walked along the fence line and mentally added that to my to-do list. Queen Anne's lace, along with a few stray thistles, dotted our path. Then I noticed something new growing near one of the posts.

I stopped my palomino gelding and loosened his reins. He grabbed some long grass and chewed it patiently while I peered at the plant. To my surprise, it was a small white oak sapling. I hated the thought of cutting it down, but it would become an issue if allowed to remain in that spot. Sighing, I nudged Blaze in the ribs with my shoes; it was just another problem to contend with. We ambled onward, trotting between our flourishing swamp oaks, ashes, and river birches until we flushed a ring-necked pheasant. Blaze startled and skidded to a stop; I managed to not take a nosedive over his shoulder. We both admired the pretty bird's flight into an adjacent bean field before heading back to the barn.

Fall harvesting, preserving produce, and building maintenance consumed most of my free hours for the rest of the season. My days off were precious, but there were a lot of chores to complete before winter descended. Occasionally to escape the stove or endless lists, I dashed down to the creek with the dogs or pedaled the beautiful bike path not far from our farm. Blaze and Red grew into their thick winter coats and enjoyed some time off. After I oiled and stored their bridles and saddles, cleared the last leaves from the gutters, and stacked the final batch of chili sauce on my basement shelves, I turned my attention to the little oak tree.

I had several free hours before the bus delivered Alex, Amie, and Hannah home. Now was the time. Clyde and I walked outside. It took a few minutes to locate my spade, and longer to find the wheelbarrow. That was in the machine shed where Hannah had left it after she used it as a chicken taxi. A cool breeze tugged at my hair and momentarily tried to distract me into catching Red for a quick tour of the neighborhood. Golden corn stalks rustled in the field as I trundled the wheelbarrow down the path along our fence line. Pulling on gloves, I grasped the spade and began to dig around the trunk of the little tree. The ground was dry and hard. Fence wires hampered shovel placement. Sweat trickled down my back.

I took a break and nibbled a granola bar, feeding the crumbs to Clyde. The hole was not deep enough yet, so I tromped back to the machine shed for a better shovel. Jake met us on the way, wagging his tail and exuding his second favorite perfume, dog-in-muddy-creek (dog-rolled-on-decayed-carcass was first.). I did not have time to investigate how he had escaped and just tied him to his usual post. Then I retrieved my garden shovel and fended off Rusty's ambush attempt.

Returning to my work area, I sighed. The little sapling stood bravely inside the chiseled earth. The little voice in my head whispered that it would be best to push the dirt back in and leave it alone. She encouraged me to catch Blaze and ride him down to the creek. Instead, I spent thirty minutes digging even deeper. Finally laying down my implement, I grasped the little tree trunk and pulled. It did not budge. How deep could that tree root have gone? Frustrated with the excavation requiring so much effort and time, I took a deep breath, leaned into the hole and cut the tap root.

Gently placing my treasure into the wheelbarrow, I quickly returned the clay and earth back into the hole. Then I threw clumps of sod on top and jumped up and down on it emphatically. Rolling the tree to its new home, I settled it in a rich mix of decayed roots and loam and watered it every day. But after two weeks, each leaf faded from vibrant green to sad brown. One by one, they withered and fell to the ground. My hasty effort to maintain perfection had destroyed a life. A gnarled oak would have added some character to the razor-straight fence line; I should have left it. The lesson reminded me to listen to that little voice of wisdom when it whispered. She had a good track record.

Chapter 39

I AWOKE WITH A START, my ears zeroing in on the unmistakable sound of a dog retching. According to the cold blue numbers of my alarm, it was three in the morning. Grabbing my robe off its hook, I quickly stumbled downstairs in the dark and arrived just in time to send Clyde out the back door before whatever decomposed critter he'd eaten ended up on the kitchen floor. At least I had not stepped in it. Sighing, I returned to bed only to be assaulted by Harry's noxious gas. Breathing through my mouth, I pushed him off the bed, opened a window, and dove under the covers before the shrill alarm beep sounded.

Ellie and Jake had been my first foray into parenthood. It was a questionable decision to proceed with human children when my canine charges never followed orders, but I figured what the heck. With the arrival of each of babies, I'd managed to juggle everyone into the mix. I was quite proud I'd never mistakenly taken one of the kids to the veterinarian instead of the pediatrician. Country life with dogs had its challenges though. Jake gobbled up cow afterbirths from the neighbor's fields and then vomited them back out once he was settled on a nice rug inside the house. Ellie loved horse manure. And Clyde required stitches several times from fighting sharp-toothed intruders.

As Jake and Ellie progressed in years, arthritis and blindness curbed their escapades. Eventually I made the decision that every pet owner dreads and sent Jake and Ellie over the rainbow bridge. I mourned for weeks. Clyde was melancholy even longer. Then a new companion for him magically came into our lives one Halloween night, when we took the kids trick-or-treating in Orangeville. Three plastic orange pumpkins overflowed with sweets after several hours of ringing doorbells, but the kids begged for one more house. That home happened to have a crate of adorable puppies on their front porch, in addition to regular size candy bars. Alex, Amie, and Hannah hit the mother lode of sugar that year, and Mom picked out a puppy. Harry was a trick, and it was on us.

The adorable puff ball grew into eighty pounds of energetic muscle. He tormented Clyde constantly. Harry drove the quest for revolting habits to a new level. His thick undercoat held odors more efficiently than any of the other dogs, thereby ensuring whatever obnoxious substance he rolled in filled the entire house with its reeking aroma. He was a card-carrying member of Carcasses Anonymous, never able to resist the siren call of maggot-infested dead things.

Two dogs just didn't seem like enough tails in the house. Amie convinced me to adopt another from the local animal shelter, and that was how Harry and Clyde met Sarah. Brindle in color, Sarah was built like a miniature grey hound. She assumed the alpha female of our pack. We taught her to smile on command: her white teeth a stark contrast to her dark coloring. Her passion was stealing socks. When she found one or two, she pranced by us with her tail high in the air, just begging for a chase. It only reinforced her bad habit.

Alex was ten, Amie eight, and Hannah six years of age respectively when the four of us attended a wedding one summer in Missouri. We came home with a puppy. The event was held at a very upscale estate, complete with an in-ground pool and heated flagstone patio. While we decorated tables for the festivities, Hannah and Amie received enthusiastic face washings from a little black and white dog. When I inquired about him during the reception, the owners happily bequeathed him to us. Jack was clever and thwarted every garbage can safety measure known.

Sadie became another addition to my No-Dog-Left-Behind program. I had recently put Clyde down and missed him terribly. En route to the pharmacy one frigid snowy morning, I spied a dog standing in an open field amid the swirling, drifting snow. By the time I drew even with it, the mutt was wading through the ditch toward the road. I pulled off onto the highway's narrow shoulder, ignoring the semi-trucks who angrily honked at me, opened the door, floundered through deep snow, and lifted her shivering body into the passenger seat. She stayed there all day while I worked. Sadie (Ditch) was ecstatic to be part of our family and showed her appreciation by destroying the couch.

Our country experiences taught us that there was a final curtain to everything: careers, childhood, seasons, and companions. Sometimes we managed to postpone an early end, but death was nothing to be afraid of. It was merely the last step to the dance we began with our first breath. It was up to us to treasure every moment in between.

Chapter 40

AS ANOTHER SUMMER FADED TO FALL, foliage transformed from weary green to brilliant yellows, oranges, and reds. The rolling hills around our farm showcased autumn's glorious colors. I didn't want to waste a day off with mowing, even though the grass in our yard was long and scraggly. After replacing the last shredded belt and duct taping the yellow seat back together, I dreaded climbing on that ancient machine. It was clear the machine was on its last season. I decided to shirk my responsibilities and visit a Madison girlfriend instead of swearing and threatening an inanimate object with a hammer for hours.

Before I met my friend at our favorite coffee shop, I detoured to the bank for some cash. Just when I rounded the corner toward the drive-up window, I slammed on the brakes. There, in the middle of my lane, stood a weathered brown rooster. He pecked at the black asphalt earnestly; obviously not the brightest thing to hatch from an egg. He hopped away from the van as I slowly pulled up to the window. As I handed the teller my withdrawal request, I asked if the bird was a new marketing ploy. She grinned and replied that he had been there when they opened; no one had claimed him.

I knew I wouldn't be able to enjoy myself while envisioning his certain demise by another driver. I turned the vehicle around and parked. All three bank employees watched through the glass as I climbed out of the van and sized up my prey. The rooster eyed me suspiciously. I slowly edged in his direction, talking in a soothing voice, and lunged at him. He easily evaded my grab.

I walked toward him again and made a quick dodge to the right. He turned left, then dashed over to the second lane. I crept behind a large bush nearby. Holding my breath, I waited. The branches rustled. Then he flew right in front of me. Reflexively, I reached and grasped what was left of his tail. He squawked and tried to slash me with his long talons. Using my other hand, I gently pressed his body to the ground until he stopped struggling. Hannah had shown me that trick. When he quieted, I picked him up and returned to the van, waving to the laughing bank employees.

The large bird was motionless in my arms during our short ride back to the farm, but I could feel his heart racing. He was a rich chocolate brown in color with iridescent blue-green tail feathers, frost-bitten wattles, and comb. I named him Valentino because he was a charmer. I pulled onto the farm lane and slowly opened my door. He kicked violently once my feet were on the ground and, in a flurry of feathers, flew from my hands.

Upon landing, Valentino cocked his head, fixed a yellow-eyed beady stare at me, and immediately ran under the front porch. Rusty, Funk, and Marge, our resident roosters, crowed in unison from their chicken coops. I placed feed and water in a couple of dishes near his hiding spot and pointed the van north again. Along the way, farmers were busy harvesting soybeans and baling the last crop of hay. Autumn was one of my favorite seasons; I loved watching the huge machines trundle through the rich black fields.

After my friend and I finished our coffee, we opted to stroll through a nearby arboretum. The visitor's center volunteer recommended an easy trail, so we grabbed our water bottles and headed down it. The sun warmed us quickly as we strolled through dried grasses and tall dead head flower stems. It was a relief when we reached the cool air of the forest. The path meandered through golden trees until it ended at a stagnant pool of water. After skirting around the foul-smelling pond, we found a different path that led us deeper into the forests.

Suddenly my stomach rumbled loudly in the middle of a quiet grove of oak trees. I looked apologetically to my friend; she laughed. It was time for lunch. At a promising fork in the path, we headed toward where we thought the parking lot was. But when we cleared the woods, there were just more gardens. I pulled out the map and discovered we were on the opposite side of the park. Too hungry to backtrack, we decided to cut through a large field with orderly rows of trees. Halfway down an aisle, I stumbled when my left foot hit a round object. I stopped and looked in the shaggy grass (they needed to mow too) for the offender. Triumphantly, I plucked the crinkled green ball from the ground. It was a hedgeapple.

I inhaled its citrus-like scent and grinned at my friend. The odd-looking fruits were inedible but prized for keeping spiders out of basements. We fanned out and searched for more. Someone else must have harvested them because mine was the only one in sight. Then we looked up. At least fifty hedge apples hung in the leafy canopy just out of reach. As my friend pondered ways to get more on the ground, I grabbed a low branch and began climbing.

Childhood memories came flooding back as I scaled the trunk. Playing hide-n-seek at night in mighty oaks, jumping out of my favorite willow into the creek below on a hot summer day, and eating mulberries while perched on a low branch in a forbidden pasture all raced through my mind. I loved climbing. Even though I was much older now, the magic of moving from limb to limb was still there. Until I reached the third branch. Ugly thorns pierced my hand. I yelped in surprise and dropped back to the ground. Blood dripped from several puncture wounds; the tree had made its position clear. No more hedgeapples for us.

My friend handed me a clean tissue to wrap around my hand, and we silently walked the border of the field until we finally found a path that led to the parking lot. I was tired, hungry, and my hand had swollen at an alarming rate. Before we got into the car, I veered off to the visitor's center and slunk by the front desk, hiding my hand behind my back until I was inside the bathroom. I didn't want to be featured under the headline of "Forty-Something Mother of Three Arrested for Climbing Protected Tree in Arboretum." After washing the blood off, I wrapped my throbbing hand in soaked paper towels, sidled past the volunteer at the desk one more time, and drove us downtown for lunch.

The waiter at the bistro looked at me oddly when I ordered their luncheon special and an ice bag, but he brought one with our drinks. I hid my hand under the table; it looked terrible. We finished our food, doing our best to ignore the rather noisy couple at the table behind us. Then I hugged my friend goodbye and headed for home.

As I waited for the kids to get off the bus, I dialed my doctor's office and booked an appointment. The kids and I shuffled into the office just before closing time. While Doc and his nurse examined my swollen hand, I sheepishly admitted how it had happened. I knew I deserved the good-natured ribbing they dished out. After all, my young children were sitting patiently in the waiting room while I was being treated for wounds from an illegal climb.

After handing me an anti-infective prescription and giving me a tetanus shot, I endured more astonished looks when we picked up my antibiotic from the pharmacy where I worked. My partner rolled his eyes; he was used to my misadventures. And our pharmacy technician grinned, handed me the medicine, and whispered she would take three hedge apples if I happened on anymore.

After rewarding my patient kids with malts from a nearby ice cream shop, we drove back home so they could do their homework. There was even enough daylight to mow the front yard. I had almost forgotten about our new rooster until Valentino appeared by the front porch steps as I jolted by on the mower. He had spotted several hens rooting through some dead leaves.

As soon as he was within ten feet of his intended, our two lead roosters converged on him. Valentino ruffled his feathers and Rusty ran behind the shed door. Funk did not back down. There was some blood lost by both parties, but our resident rooster dominated. As I put the mower away, Valentino retreated to just outside the zone Funk established. When the chickens returned to their roosts at dusk, Valentino withdrew to a basement windowsill under the front porch.

Valentino's crows reverberated through the living room floor before dawn every morning. His demeanor was extremely aggressive. Our hens despised him; he was brutal and strong. The kids and I carried chicken sticks whenever we were outside to fend off his attacks. I realized that he would never be grateful for his rescue in the drive-thru that day and gave him to a neighbor looking for a guard rooster. Valentino filled the role admirably.

As I bounced through our back yard on the mower the following week, I pondered the lessons I'd learned that day: 1) not all stray animals appreciate a good home, 2) climbing thorny trees in an arboretum is not a great idea, 3) and sometimes bad decisions make the best stories.

Chapter 41

THE FOUL FOWL EXPERIENCE with Valentino didn't deter me from other animal rescue missions. He had found a home after I saved him from the bank drive-thru; it just wasn't ours. For some odd reason, I was a magnet to animals and fowl in need. So, I wasn't surprised one evening when the quintessential question of "Why did the chicken cross the road?" presented its answer: she was looking for me.

Driving along a busy highway to a banquet, I sang along loudly to a melody on the radio. I grinned, remembering my youngest's query regarding the last song I had stumbled through the night before. "Mom, who sings this song?" she had asked. I had answered with the name of the artist. "Let's keep it that way," she had said.

Suddenly the truck braked in front of me. I slammed on my brakes to avoid crashing into him. Midwest drivers were on edge; it was deer hunting season and panicked animals fleeing shotgun blasts often met their demise with a bumper. But there were no tan long-legged fugitives within sight. Then a small brown form darted out in front of my car. It was a chicken. Her frightened eye met mine for a second before she scurried to the other side of the ditch.

Cars honked angrily. I gradually accelerated and weighed my options. If I turned around to make sure the hen was safe, I would be late. But that was better than being haunted by her deer-in-the-headlights stare. Resolutely, I turned around and drove back to the scene. The chicken pecked at some weeds near a blacktop driveway, so I pulled into it and got out of the car slowly. She immediately ran toward the house, where the garage door was open. I poked my head inside and called, "Hello?" A man was welding several pieces of metal in the corner, but he did not hear me until I shouted. Then he jumped. Wiping his grease-stained hands on a shop towel, he tilted his mask up. I smiled at him awkwardly, pointed at the hen, and asked, "Is that your chicken?"

He nodded. "She ran across the road in front of me," I told him. His wife appeared in the doorway. As I relayed my story again, she sighed. The little chicken was the sole survivor of four babies they had raised that summer. The owners had no fowl experience; they purchased the chicks thinking it would be nice to have fresh eggs. They hadn't known about raccoons, owls, and coyotes. I explained that we kept a small but well-loved flock on our farm. Simultaneously they asked me if I would take her. "Of course" was my reflexive response.

The husband dug out a large fishing net from a corner of the garage, but the chicken easily dodged his efforts. The three of us circled around her, cutting her off when she tried to head back to the cars and trucks whizzing past. I kicked off my sandals to negotiate the rough ground better. After twenty minutes, I was sweaty, and my good clothes were stained from a near miss that ended in a slide my old softball coach would have been proud of. But as the sun dipped lower in the sky, our runaway slowed her pace and found refuge in a tree.

I worked my way through the spruce branches until I could reach her tail feathers. She squawked loudly as I carefully pulled her out, but quieted as I cradled her in my scratched and bleeding arms. The couple loaned me a small crate which I promised to return. I placed the chicken tenderly inside and loaded it into the backseat. I waved goodbye as the couple stood in the driveway and set off for my event again. After parking in the bowling alley lot, I told the hen I'd be back and headed into the banquet hall, pulling what I hoped was the last pine needle from my hair.

I found the seat my friends had saved me, grabbed a plate, and filled it with food. Between forkfuls of salad and mashed potatoes, I explained why I was late. They all shook their heads and chuckled. They invited the chicken inside, but I declined; they probably intended to cook her.

After the program, I drove my new acquisition home. Hannah quickly plucked the hen from my arms when I brought her into the farmhouse. I dug through the refrigerator and found some squishy grapes in the back. We fed her the snack and named her Grace after the song I'd been listening to on the radio. A full moon illuminated the buildings as we carried her out to the coop.

Our flock was roosting in their shed. Hannah placed the new hen near the feeder and bucket of water. Grace fixed her beady orange eye on us, nibbled some cracked corn, and drank a little water. Then she hopped up onto the rail next to Rusty like she had lived there her whole life. Her decision to cross the road had been a good one.

Chapter 42

ALEX, AMIE, AND HANNAH GAZED OUT at the lead gray sky through the living room window. Ice storms were a hazard in the Midwest, especially late autumn. I looked at the clock and wondered if the bus had slid into the ditch again, pondering the sensibility of driving them to school myself. If the roads were so slick that the heavy bus could not make it up the hills, our old blue van was destined for failure. I secretly hoped they would cancel school, giving me some unscheduled bonus time to spend with my brood.

Living in the country made me comfortable with the fact that I did not fit the standard mother model. Fewer people equaled lower pressure to conform. My lone wolf trait of pursuing unusual activities like painting murals on barns and riding my bicycle fifty miles was able to express itself freely out in the middle of nowhere. Trashy romance novels on the porch swing defeated window cleaning every time.

I rejoiced in my rediscovered personal space once toddlers no longer clung desperately to my legs, but already missed thier young voices echoing through the farmhouse. Toys no longer littered my hardwood floors; they had been replaced by the buzz of dial up internet. I was shocked to wake up one day to discover Alex reading car magazines and Amie shaving her legs. There had to be a way to spend some quality one-on-one time with each of them instead of the parental zone defense I continually applied.

Looking out the window at the dark rich fields that fateful morning, a light bulb flashed on in my head. There were plenty of teachable moments outside the brick walls of their school. Skipping school one day a year wouldn't harm them. Each child would choose how they wanted to spend our day together. It would be twelve hours where I could devote my entire attention to them as individuals. The kids enthusiastically embraced the proposal as they ate their oatmeal, and we all cheered when the radio announced school had been cancelled.

After breakfast, we huddled around the kitchen table with mugs of steaming hot chocolate. Skip dates were marked for each child on the refrigerator calendar, giving them time to think about what they wanted to do. I smiled as they tossed marshmallows to the dogs hovering at our knees. Amie won the "guess how long it takes for Harry's drool to drop to the floor" contest, accompanied by groans of disgust from Alex and Hannah. I grabbed a towel.

For Alex's holidays, we traveled to Midwest ski resorts so he could hone his snowboarding skills. In a short span of time, he transformed from a beginner to capable boarder. Jumps and rails in the terrain parks helped perfect his art and multiplied my worries. He turned out to be a patient instructor as I struggled to master my own snowboard and rolled his eyes when I fell at the chair lift every time.

Amie chose to spend her skip day shopping. At the mall, we strolled from store to store where I marveled at the ridiculously high expense of teen clothes. She pirouetted in fancy dresses and heels outside the dressing rooms. Sometimes I even tried on a few, and our giggles were hard to hear over rustling layers of taffeta and lace. Lunch was always at a nice restaurant. A movie rounded out our day, complete with popcorn, soda, and candy.

Hannah decided indoor water parks in the Wisconsin Dells were her style. We left early in the morning with a cooler full of snacks and a waterproof camera to record our days. After splashing and laughing in inner tubes along the lazy river, we rode waves in the big pool for a while. Once we were both waterlogged, we changed into real clothes and drove off in search of an eatery before returning home.

The bonds and memories I forged with my children while sharing those adventures buoyed me through the next era of teenagers testing their wings and my rules. Alex, Amie, and Hannah held up their end of the bargain for skip day beautifully; their grades never faltered.

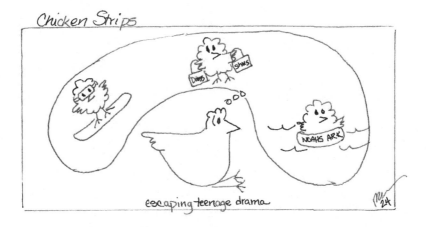

Chapter 43

THE PHARMACIST SHORTAGE hit rural areas hard. An old college classmate called me one day with an opportunity thirty minutes from the farm. He was the manager for a small chain and needed a pharmacist in one of their stores. The shifts were longer, but I would have a four-day work week instead of shifts that varied month to month. And the prescription volume was half of my current workload. I accepted his offer and gave my two-week notice joyfully.

Working in a small town was much less stressful. It was fun getting to know the community. After a few months, everyone knew I often commuted to work on my bike in the summer, snowboarded with my son in the winter, and owned a farm filled with cast-off animals. My livestock adventures quickly became a rich source of entertainment for farmers at their early morning coffee gatherings.

One of my patients asked me if I was in the market for more chickens one morning. I looked up from my stack of unchecked prescriptions, ignored the telephone's jangling, and craned my head around the corner to see if he was serious. He was. I inwardly sighed because whatever he was about to propose would most likely cause me more work and money. I took a deep breath, and cautiously replied, "Maybe…" He began his story.

There was a historical settlement in a nearby community. Reenactments of civil war skirmishes were popular events there, and the old log buildings displayed costumes and belongings from that era. The fort also kept chickens in the summer as part of the pioneer setting but did not have adequate facilities to support them through the harsh Midwest winters. My customer had learned that six hens remained from the summer's flock and were from a rare breed that had been hatched in a Chicago Museum. The girls either needed a new home or a large stew pot.

I knew what my answer should be. Egg sales did not begin to cover the cost of feed, and our roosts were already crowded. But a vision of any hen de-feathered and poised over a boiling pot of water forced my hand. I told my customer I would take in a few as I handed him his medicine. He happily gave me the contact person's number.

On my next day off, I called the fort's caretaker about the chickens. She invited me to the facility. Hannah and I set off on our quest after the bus dropped the kids off one dismal October day. Alex and Amie stayed home to play video games. Raindrops splattered the windshield; I glanced back at the cage in the rear of the van to make sure I had not forgotten it. The western skyline was dark and ominous. My youngest daughter and I plotted where we should settle the new hens when we returned while the wire crate in the back rattled.

Rusty, Grace, and the original clan still resided in the original coop. A younger group of chickens, prodigy of Betty (a Phoenix hen) lived in the bottom level of our big barn. They were governed by Marge, a small, sneaky rooster. He was probably angry about his name; we had not known "she" was "he" upon hatching. Hannah had witnessed his last attack against me: I'd whacked him a little too hard with a stick. Reviving him did not improve his temperament. Considering Marge's lack of compassion, we decided any new residents would have a better chance with the older, kinder group.

We drove through steady rain. At times I could barely see the white lines marking the road edge. Arriving just before closing time, I parked in the lot close to the exhibit hall. The rain soaked us before we made it to the door, held open by the caretaker who held an umbrella. Our coats dripped water onto the old wooden floors as she gave us a brief introduction to the center. Because the fort was a non-profit organization, she needed to document where the hens were placed. It was at that moment that I realized we were owners to six new chickens, not just two like we originally planned. Subconsciously, I guess I had known that all along and signed without protest. We returned to our vehicle and followed her truck as it splashed up a winding lane to an ancient wooden shed.

She held her umbrella over my head as I hoisted our cage inside. Hannah carried a flashlight and shone it into the corners. The hens peered down at us but thankfully stayed on their roosts within easy reach. One by one, I grabbed them and popped their plump bodies into the crate. Hannah named the large red hen Charlotte; my daughter held her as I struggled to make room in the crowded cage. Hannah begged to hold her on the way home, but visions of a loose chicken flying around inside our vehicle were not pretty. She went in the heavy cage with the others. Hannah and I thanked the caretaker and waved goodbye as we drove away.

The windshield wipers squeaked in unison while Hannah excitedly reeled off names for the rest of the birds. Snowflakes appeared and then melted. The hens clucked softly. We pulled into a fast-food drive through and ordered sandwiches; both of us were starving. But we did not linger after receiving the sack of burgers and fries; a pungent ammonia odor floated from the back of the vehicle to the front. I was glad we had put down a tarp under the cage. We choked down our food and breathed through our mouths as the miles passed.

After we parked in front of our coop, Hannah and I lugged the heavy chickens through the door and set the cage down in the middle of the floor. We unlatched and opened the door, but the hens were so tightly packed they couldn't move. I pulled them out one by one. They shook out their feathers and huddled together in a corner. Rusty and his gang looked down at the newcomers but did not move from their roosts. The newcomers nibbled at some cracked corn, and then one by one flew onto the lowest open bar to roost. We closed the door softly.

Over the next few weeks, a new pecking order was established. Rusty considered the new additions to his harem an early Christmas gift. The pretty hens added brown and blue eggs in return for their nice new home. Charlotte was the tamest chicken, and always begged for treats when it was feeding time. Our previous favorites welcomed the break from constant attention; Feather regrew her tail feathers and Rusty's hot pink nail polish faded. Charlotte and Grace became the best of friends and always wandered our farm together. Our chickens taught us that no matter how crowded the coop, there was always room for more (plus they had no sense of calendar time.)

Chicken Strips

Chapter 44

STORMY SILENCE FILLED THE VAN as we pulled up to the drive-thru window. I needed fifteen more cents to pay for three orders of chicken tenders. Spying a quarter wedged between the cup holders, I dug it out and handed it along with crumpled dollar bills to the small hand reaching toward me. Cold air rushed into van, and I glanced at the rear-view mirror filled with the sullen faces of my children. They weren't getting shakes or sodas, merely the food. I had just paid the annual propane contract and purchased winter hay for the horses; there was very little in the budget for frivolous expenses like eating out.

Our silver maple trees had dropped their yellow and brown leaves overnight. Flocks of geese winged their way south over the farm in large "V" formations. Getting ready for winter occupied my free time. I stored my saddles and bridles in the barn and set up the horse waterer with a de-icer. Heat lamps were hung in the coops. Covering the straw bales over the well pit lid with plastic trash bags prevented them from soaking up fifty extra pounds of rain. In the pit itself, my father suggested a 100-watt light bulb along with our portable heater to provide warmth and light in the dark space.

After waxing my snowboard, I scheduled weekly checks of the water system on our refrigerator calendar. I really didn't want a repeat of frozen pipes or tanks. A plank over the hole in the shed floor prevented the chickens in the coop from falling in, and when moved aside gave me a clear view of the underground room. Snow accumulated on the wrapped bales to further insulate the well pit, and water continued to flow into the house and horse shed.

The twenty-year-old furnace that squatted in the corner of our limestone basement had dramatically increased its appetite for propane over the last few winters. There were two possible causes: either the kids secretly shifted the thermostat setting higher when I was gone, or it was just too tired to keep up with our drafty, poorly insulated house. When I mentioned it to my father, he recommended I change the filter. One morning I trudged downstairs and looked through the ragged owner's manual. After dusting off the cobwebs, I gripped the filter's frame and pulled. It did not budge.

Muttering to myself, I retrieved a pair of pliers. With those and a lot more muscle, it suddenly released. I fell backward on the cement floor, clutching my prize.

Even with my un-experienced eyes, I could not imagine air molecules finding a path through that blackened mesh. After replacing it with a new disposable filter, the furnace refused to send out anything but weak little puffs of warm air. My father recommended I have the unit checked out, but his sound advice was forgotten between monitoring the homework for three kids, cooking raspberry jam from frozen berries in the freezer, and days checking prescriptions.

One frigid January night, I finally realized it was not normal to go to bed with four layers of clothes and huddle under the covers next to three dogs just to stay warm. The kids had electric baseboard heat in their bedrooms, so they slept well, but the rest of the house was freezing. I called my father in sunny Florida to get the contact information for the heating company he used. When the salesman took my call, I explained our situation and begged him to send a technician as soon as possible.

The repairman's arrival was heralded by a blast of arctic air when he opened the mud porch door. My guard dogs were still curled up on my bed and did not bother sounding the alarm until his voice drifted upstairs. I was baking bread, cookies, and anything else I could think of just to keep the kitchen warm. Two minutes later he called me downstairs. I peered over his shoulder into the unit.

"You see that?" he asked.

"See what?" I responded.

He nodded. "Exactly," he said. There was no blue flame in the burner to generate heat. The poor old furnace was just re-circulating cold air from the basement into the house. Several thousand dollars later, a new unit quietly purred in its corner and sent warm air through the vents. The unit paid for itself in two years with its lower fuel costs. Even though I did not need their body heat anymore, I still let the dogs sleep with me. Sadly, a broken furnace wasn't the only winter problem surfacing that month.

One frosty morning, I gathered eggs to make crepes as a surprise breakfast for the kids. As I reached beneath Feather to retrieve several warm ovals, I heard an odd gurgling sound coming from the well pit underneath the chicken coop. A bad feeling settled in the pit of my stomach. I scurried outside, tugged the straw bales away from the lid, lifted the insulated wooden cover and peered down into the dark room. Water sprayed like a fountain from a valve on the side of the holding tank and was pooling on the dirt floor. If the murky liquid reached the well casing, our entire water supply would be contaminated again. My surprise breakfast was canceled. Swinging my foot onto the top of the little step ladder I had left in the pit, I lowered myself down.

Cold water sprayed my face as I examined the bolts near the suspect valve. I had no idea what to do to fix it, so I stepped back up onto the ladder, climbed out of the pit, and headed for the basement where the emergency sump pump was. Dragging it upstairs and through the kitchen, I said good morning to the kids. They were fighting over who got the last bowl of cereal; losers ate oatmeal. Sighing, I dragged my equipment outside with the hose clanking behind. The little voice in my head whispered that it was slightly disturbing that Alex, Amie, and Hannah saw nothing out of the ordinary with my actions. Were my frequent battles with Mother Nature going to come out in therapy someday? I shuffled back outside, fished the suction part down into pit and plugged the pump in. As it sent black water out the hose behind the coop, I realized the little machine wasn't going keep up with the leak.

Racing back inside the house, I made a panicked call to my plumber. Filthy water pooled on the kitchen floor around my boots. He answered the telephone and calmly told me I'd be their first stop. He recommended shutting off electricity to the well until they arrived, which would depressurize the tank and stop the water flow. My resourceful and independent children were ready for their day, finishing up homework at the table. I blew them kisses from the back door and dashed back outside.

There was a power switch in a dark corner of the pit, directly under the chicken coop. Climbing back down into the pit, I sloshed past the whining pump and followed the wires from the well pump to a grey metal box covered with cobwebs. Dusting it off with my soaked glove, I found the rusty switch. Tiptoeing to the driest point possible, I pulled it down. Blackness descended in the room once more, but the holding tank depressurized with a long hissing noise. Groping my way back to the ladder, I wearily climbed out and trudged to the house.

When my plumber arrived, the pit was relatively dry. The little pump had worked well. I fished the intake out, drained the hose, and put everything in the feed shed attached to the barn while he dragged parts and connections to the pit. I shivered on the ledge and handed him tools as he replaced the defective float valve. When he turned the electric back on, no more water sprayed. After he crawled back out of the pit, he helped me replace the straw bales over the lid and recommended a new holding tank. The one I had was at least twenty years old. I mentally added that to my wish list, right after braces for all three of my kids.

Chicken Strips

Chapter 45

THE MIST FROM MY BREATH hovered in the frigid air. Snow squeaked beneath my boots along the shoveled path to the chicken shed. Harry trotted in front of me, stopping to sniff and mark his usual spots. Shivering in my barn coat and insulated coveralls, I lifted the latch to the door and clicked on the light switch. Moving quietly among chickens that were fluffed to twice their normal size, I poured feed into the feeder and checked the water. It was frozen.

I paused to stroke a feathered head here and there as Charlotte waddled up to me for the bread crust I carried in my pocket for her. I counted beaks after plugging in the heated water bucket and warming lamp. We should have turned them on the day before. All hens were present and accounted for, but Rusty was unusually silent. Even though he was an idiot, I enjoyed watching our white leghorn saunter around the farm. His crowing was so boisterous that he often fell from precarious perches. I finally spotted him in a corner, alone.

Approaching him cautiously, I noticed that his wattles and comb were discolored and swollen. He did not fight me when I picked him up and just stood listlessly beside the feed and water when I set him underneath the heat lamp. After sending the kids off to school, I checked on Rusty periodically. No improvement.

I called several veterinarians and skimmed through our chicken guidebooks. There was no information on treating a frost-bitten rooster. When his red comb took on a blue hue, I knew immediate action was necessary. Bundled in layers of outerwear, I trudged up to the barn to retrieve the spare crate we had used to transport Charlotte and her friends. I filled it with fresh straw and carried it to the house.

Leaving a trail of yellow twigs behind me, I wrestled the heavy cage into the kitchen. The dogs sniffed it, then promptly chose their hiding spots just in case it was for them. I went back out to the coop to capture my patient, who was delirious in a chicken coma. Carrying him close to protect him from the wind, I waded through the frozen tundra of our yard. A gust of wind slammed the door shut behind us.

Staring at that miserable lump of feathers, I racked my brain for ideas. Maybe he needed water. So, I dug a medicine dropper out of the cupboard, filled a cup, and forced a little liquid into his beak. His wattles were so huge he could not hold his head up, so I cradled him in my arms. He swallowed reflexively while staring glassily into space.

Reasoning antibiotics might help, I added tetracycline powder to the water and administered one dropper full every hour. After the school bus dropped off my kids, Hannah was devastated by the appearance of her favorite rooster. She took frequent breaks from her math homework to help. None of us really wanted to leave him to attend the grade school winter concert that night, but I dragged all three protesting children into the van. We returned home as quickly as possible.

Rusty was still alive the next morning. Knowing he had not eaten for several days, Hannah and I wetted chicken feed and used a small spoon to guide it down his gullet. It was incredibly messy, but I promised Hannah I would keep the schedule of feeding and watering every hour while she and her siblings were at school. On the second morning of Rusty's hospitalization, we noticed his wattles had shrunken significantly. Some of the old glare was back in his yellow eyes, and he struggled so much at feeding time that chicken mash flew all over us and the floor. He was ready to eat and drink on his own. After experimenting with several designs for makeshift feeders, we cut holes in paper cups and attached them to the cage with twist ties. They worked perfectly.

By the third day, his crows reverberated throughout the house. Several friends questioned my sanity when they heard him in the background over the telephone. Amie and Alex complained after he woke them up at four in the morning, and the sharp odor of chicken manure had permeated our home. It was time for him to rejoin the brood.

Hannah and I carried him back out to the coop in the afternoon. The little building was warmer than our house after the addition of a portable heater and a second heat lamp. After some initial scuffling, Rusty meekly settled onto a roosting bar between Feather and Charlotte. Once he regained his strength, he enthusiastically attacked my calves whenever I did chores. But I didn't mind. It was good to have my rebel rooster back after his tango with death's icy grip.

Rusty's Spicy Raspberry Pepper Jam

2 c. raspberries
½ c. cider vinegar
6 c. sugar

1 pkg fruit pectin
8 red jalepeno peppers
2 red bell peppers

Prepare water bath & sterilize jars and lids. Finely chop peppers, mix in vinegar and raspberries with scant ½ c. water. Follow recipe for cooked jams on pectin box, adding sugar as directed. Process filled jars for recommended time.

This jam tastes great with cream cheese on crackers!

Chapter 46

ONE NIGHT, A FIERCE WIND suddenly gusted through the front porch and rocked me violently in the hammock. An early spring storm had descended upon my little farm. Disoriented, it took me a few minutes to remember I had fallen asleep outside. Harry nervously paced nearby. Freeing my blanket from where it was wedged between several rails, I carried it into the house. Harry followed at my heels.

The clock on the stove flashed neon green characters. No power. Feeling my way along the walls to the stairs and up into my bedroom, lightning flashes illuminated the trembling forms of Sadie and Jack huddled on my comforter. I chided them for being so fearful and crawled into bed between them. I heard Harry barking by the coop, but I was so exhausted I fell into a deep sleep.

A rogue raccoon had recently taken up residence in our barn. Harry spent hours barking and sniffing the second level, but that coon evaded him skillfully. The masked bandit treated himself to a fresh chicken dinner at will, no matter how well I barricaded and reinforced the coops. Stray feathers from the missing bird were the only evidence the villain left behind. Charlotte was his first victim. Betty disappeared the next week. When I discovered Grace's feathers, I declared war.

My affection for farm animals ran deep, but rural life put us in intimate contact with the circle of life. Everyone was food for someone else. Kittens were carried off by coyotes, and occasional minks devoured a few hens until the dogs fought them off. I understood some losses were unavoidable, but that didn't stop my "mama bear" instincts. Losing any more of my flock to this new four-pawed threat was not an option.

The raccoon easily evaded my carefully laid live traps. Desperate to save the few egg-laying chickens and guardian roosters remaining, I spent my entire weekend off patching every hole and crevice where the chickens roosted. All was quiet for a few weeks. Then one rainy evening I sent Hannah out to the barn to gather eggs. She did not want to go alone, but Amie was at a friend's house and Alex was helping a friend work on a car. I shooed her outside with the basket and flashlight. Thirty seconds later she reappeared at the kitchen door, flushed, frantic, and out of breath.

"There is something chasing Oreo," she gasped. I threw on my coat and raced out the door, leaving a chicken pot pie (not one of ours) in the oven. Harry ran ahead of me. I heard squawking as I unbolted the barn door. Scanning the room under the flickering glow of fluorescent lights, I finally spotted the bird. He was our youngest rooster and had lost one eye during a nasty battle with Marge. Now his black and white speckled feathers were scattered everywhere.

I picked up a stray broom handle and approached a bunch of wooden planks and plywood pieces stacked against the southern wall. Harry stood before it, growling with raised hackles. Cautiously I began moving the boards out of the way. Glancing back at Hannah, I asked her to fetch the shovel. She returned a few minutes later with a large heavy stick. Then she climbed up onto a wooden work bench.

Taking a deep breath, I patted Harry on the back and pulled the last board away from the wall. When the haze of dust settled, the largest raccoon I had ever seen reared up on its hind legs defiantly. Harry pounced, grabbed it by the neck and gave it a strong shake. When my dog let go, I stepped forward but the raccoon backed into a corner where it was hard to reach.

The raccoon lunged upward. I tried to get a clear angle as the enraged animal clung to Harry's belly. They both careened toward me. My big dog yelped as the raccoon's teeth found their mark. Harry shook the animal off, and the raccoon snarled as I stepped between them. White hot anger coursed through my veins as I held the stick ready. Suddenly the raccoon spun around and lumbered outside.

We grabbed Oreo and settled him on a counter, then walked back to the farmhouse. A cold rain began to fall. Harry sported several deep oozing scratches; I cleaned them while Hannah turned off the oven and pulled out the spaghetti pie I'd been baking. But neither of us were hungry, so we cut a generous slice for Harry and put the rest in the refrigerator. We sat at the kitchen table; I sipped chamomile tea and Hannah layered whipped cream onto her hot chocolate. She never went to the barn alone after that night. I didn't blame her.

Chapter 47

FARMING IN OUR LITTLE CORNER of the Midwest was a community effort. Everyone needed help occasionally, whether it was weeding rows of organic corn plants or corralling errant cows. And sometimes rural animals needed help, like a goat caught in a wire fence (it happened on a bike ride to work one day) or a young heifer who got herself in a bad position. The latter occurred one evening as I was headed to opening night for the high school musical. For months Amie had been practicing diligently with the cast in her role as chorus girl, and I couldn't wait to see her on stage. I had just enough time to rush home and change clothes before the curtain rose.

Small patches of bright green grass poked through waves of snow in the ditches. I was itching to get my bicycle tuned and retrieve the horses' saddles and tack from storage. Turning the van onto the main road, I pondered if Blaze needed a different bit since the veterinarian had removed some of his teeth when my gaze was drawn to a small cow lying in a neighbor's pasture. She lifted her head slightly as I drove by.

Something seemed off. Did I have time to turn around and make sure she was alright? I glanced in my rear-view mirror. She had not moved, and there was no herd in sight. I sighed, turned the truck around, and parked at the edge of the gravel road. I wasn't exactly dressed for field work but opened the door and got out anyway.

After crossing the road, I struggled through the ditch on the other side where drifts were two feet deep. Snow slid into my boots and melted down toward my toes. When I reached the mesh fence with two strands of barbed wire on the top, I tapped it cautiously. No zaps. Placing one foot on a strand two feet from the ground, I slowly swung my other leg over and grimaced at the accompanying ripping noise. Yanking my skirt free, I dropped to the other side and walked toward the animal. The heifer lifted her head from the mud, and I gently scratched her broad face. It looked like she had been struggling for a while.

She laid on just enough of an incline that she could not get her legs underneath for leverage. She was too big to roll over. Bovine bloat was a danger to cows who couldn't move; it required immediate attention. After pacing back and forth, I thought that if I wiggled her around, she might be able to get to her feet. Taking a deep breath, I grabbed her front legs and gently pulled them. She slid easily on the still frozen ground. Then I moved to her back legs and did the same. After going back and forth for ten minutes, I had her in a spot where she looked like she could get up on her knees. Catching my breath, I patted her nose and scratched between her ears.

I clapped my hands and stood back. She just raised her head and looked at me curiously. I stomped the ground and jumped up and down. She rolled her eyes at me. Finally, I gave her a strong push. She grunted and contracted one front leg beneath her. Then the other. She pushed her back legs into the snow. Then, as I climbed back out over the same section of fence, the young cow shakily rose to her feet. She stared back at me with her big brown eyes as if to say thank you and then trotted off to find her companions. I smiled and waded through the ditch back to the truck.

My feet were frozen, but my heart was warm. There was no time to change clothes, so I drove straight to the high school. I paid for the admission and hustled into the gymnasium, finding a seat near my friends just as the lights dimmed. Up on the stage, amid beautifully painted settings, the actors and chorus line performed. I was captivated by the efforts of the cast, crew, and director. After several standing ovations, I stood in line to congratulate everyone. Not one word was said about the ragged hole in my skirt as I praised the actors and actresses and hugged Amie tightly. She had done a wonderful job, and I was very proud—of both of us.

Chicken Strips

Chapter 48

THE PHYSICAL ASPECTS OF FARM MAINTENANCE helped balance the mental challenges of pharmacy and parenting teenagers. Sometimes the constant battles with Mother Nature and buildings intent on returning to the earth was overwhelming. Hours of whitewashing weathered wood and pounding nails into window frames threatening to fall made a cute little bungalow in town with a small, fenced yard seem quite attractive. But I stubbornly held onto my country dream.

Scrapbooking was on my agenda one day. After stacking the last mug into the dishwasher, I walked into the dining room to begin working on Alex's book. The ground was still frozen and covered with four inches of fresh snow from an early spring storm. Leaden skies delivered steady pouring rains that slowed for brief interludes before mounting torrential attacks again. The kids were all at friends' houses that had better electronics. Sadie, Sarah, Jack, and Harry had staked out spots on the living room floor to nap in.

Raindrops drummed on the metal cellar doors as I went down into the basement searching for my scissors. Hannah had used them last on a project for school that required more room than our dining room table.

She had set up all her materials in the back room which was pretty level. I picked up the scissors from the floor and turned to go back upstairs. But when I glanced in my pantry, a dark pool of water was quickly growing on its cement floor. Photo albums were forgotten.

It had been a while since I had used the bilge pump for the well pit. I vaguely remembered seeing it somewhere on the mud porch. Trotting upstairs, I found it hanging on the northern wall. The long hose slithered behind me, bouncing down each step with a clank as I carried it downstairs. I set the pump on top of a five-gallon bucket, primed it, and set the triangular inlet in the pool. Then I dragged the outlet hose out the cellar doors and placed it far enough away from the house so the effluent wouldn't flow right back inside.

I realized that if there was that much water in the basement, the well pit was probably in imminent danger as well. Donning my insulated coveralls and boots, I shuffled outside to wrestle the bags of straw away from the well pit lid. I'd used those instead of bales; they were lighter and easier to move. After lifting the well pit cover, I peered down into the underground room. Sure enough, there was black water oozing toward the well inlet, but it had not risen to the contamination point yet. I needed to pump both areas simultaneously, but I only had one pump. Running the pump from one area to the other became the urgent task of the day.

After hauling everything outside, I angled the suction end down into the pit and set the pump on another bucket under the over-hang of the barn. I stood inside the feed shed to avoid the cold rain and contemplated driving to town to get a more powerful pump. But if I left, the well would be full of mud by the time I returned. I needed to make do. Once the pit level lowered enough to be out of the danger zone, I unplugged the machine and dragged it back into the basement. Sadie ran past me up the steps and merrily raced around the yard. I let her go; maybe the rain would wash out whatever she found to roll in.

I lost count of how many trips I made stumbling through the slush, shuttling equipment back and forth between the two locations. I was soaked, miserable, and cold. The clouds above me and inside my head continued their attack. Sadie returned with her tail between her back legs, reeking of dead possum. I let her inside, too tired to care if she rubbed her stinky self against the couch. After snarling at the dogs to fix their own lunch when they begged to be fed, I felt guilty. My flooded situation was not their fault.

Gritting my teeth, I cursed the wind as it whipped stinging drops at me. I had to stay calm and keep a level head to stay afloat, literally. But what if the same thing happened while I was away at work one day? Sadie or Jack could not be trained to operate even a simple switch; they spent all day chasing sparrows in the barn. I needed an option that did not require clucking over water levels like a mother hen during every storm. There had to be a solution to my water woes.

After eight hours of slipping and sliding on the ice and through the mud, a small break in the clouds appeared. The stream in the basement slowed to a trickle, the well pit flood receded, and I felt a twinge of something that felt like hope. The kids baked a frozen pizza and cleaned up after themselves without being nagged. Both areas were finally free from standing water as night descended.

I placed the pump back in the garage, tossed my boots on the porch and peeled my filthy outerwear off into a pile. Stumbling upstairs, I drew marvelously clear water for a hot bath and soaked for thirty minutes in rosemary-scented salts. After I crawled into bed, Amie and Hannah delivered a tray of leftover pizza and hot chocolate. I devoured everything as they sat on my bed and filled me in on current happenings at school. Their lives revolved around boys, best friends, and movies instead of well pits and basements. They left after a while, no doubt needing to text their friends something vitally important.

A few minutes later, Alex strolled into my room and threw his lanky form down on the chair next to my bed. His nose disappeared into the second volume of the series he was immersed in. I was too tired to take my dishes downstairs, so I put them on the floor where Sadie and Jack licked them clean. Falling asleep after three pages of my trashy romance novel, I dreamed of a shopping spree featuring two high-capacity pumps with easy to carry handles—and a cute bag filled with brightly patterned underwear.

After that, I began monitoring the well pit periodically during heavy rains. It wasn't unusual for me to spend hours standing in the rain pumping water from that dank little underground room. Harry stood by my side faithfully every time. We kept an eye out for my fairy godmother. I still had hopes that someday she would wave her magic wand and make all my water woes disappear. Much more useful than glass slippers. But I would not say no to a cute pair of heels if they were part of the package.

Chapter 49

FINDING A SERVICE OPPORTUNITY for my family was an important goal. I wanted to instill the idea of giving back to my children, even if it couldn't always be monetary. We helped with occasional community projects and volunteered at the Madison Ironman Triathlon every year. But I yearned for something else.

Anything that involved more effort than foraging for food in the brightly lit refrigerator or exercising their fingers on remote controls usually met with strong vocal resistance from my three. Still, the idea simmered in the back of my mind. Then a solution appeared one day as we drove into the suburbs of Chicago for our annual summer expedition. Adopt-a-Highway signs were posted frequently along the expressway. One with a family name caught my eye, and I realized it was the perfect undertaking for us.

Once we arrived safely back at the farm, I accessed the Illinois highway web site, filled out the form, sent it electronically, and did not breathe a word of my plan to the unsuspecting adolescents enjoying their summer. After several weeks of waiting, our dusty mailbox produced an official-looking envelope containing paperwork and a training video. We were an official sponsor of one mile of Illinois highway, responsible for picking up trash along our designated stretch four times a year. Eagerly, I called the local IDOT office to obtain supplies.

The initial date I chose turned out to be a sweltering August day. Undaunted by the loud protests of my almost-adult children, I informed Alex and Amie that we indeed would be following through on our commitment (Hannah was spending the weekend elsewhere). A desperate attempt to find friends to help them suffer through the task ensued. Amie managed to trick one classmate into coming along; I discovered in the van on the way back to the farm that my child had not disclosed the true purpose of our mission. Their complaints of sudden headaches and stomach pains fell on deaf ears.

At the farm, Alex and I loaded the box filled with equipment into the back of the van. Then we watched the safety video. It was entertaining and informative. The girls tried to delay with emergency wardrobe changes. Alex and I sat in the vehicle and honked the horn until they finally appeared. I sighed. Instead of the happy crew I had envisioned working together to clean up a small part of our world, I was now the leader of a prison gang, several of whom just wanted to escape.

I played my trump card, bribery. After promising cold drinks and snacks at the gas station once our work was done, we pulled over to the side of the road under the sign that identified the beginning of our stewardship. Then we climbed out of the vehicle into oppressive humidity. I opened the box and handed everyone a vest. The appalled looks I received from the girls wiped out all positive vibes from the bribe. While Alex and I donned the oversized neon vests and grabbed several orange trash bags, the girls experimented with various methods of attaching the unfashionable garments to their bodies without wearing them.

While they fussed with their outfits, Alex and I began walking along the roadside side by side. One of us picked up refuse with gloved hands while the other held the bag open. The girls finally tied the orange vests around their arms, picked up their bags, and began to move very slowly on the other side of the highway. I observed Amie struggling to text and carry her trash bag at the same time.

In companionable silence, Alex and I made our way toward the other sign that marked the end of our adopted mile. Sweat dripped own my back, and I wished I had brought a bottle of water along. We picked up aluminum beer cans, plastic bottles beheaded by the ditch mowers, and shredded candy bar wrappers, but the most prevalent pieces of garbage were countless wrappers and cups from fast food franchises. The massive amount of trash we gathered was shocking. Amie and her friend were a least a hundred yards behind us and sitting down to rest.

Cars whizzed by us, occasionally honking their horns. Amie waved at them (another excuse to not work). The bags Alex and I carried grew heavier as we scanned the tall weeds. Our silence was punctuated by frequent buzzing that alerted him to new text messages. My legs itched, and I made a mental note to wear long pants the next time.

After almost an hour of stopping, bending, stooping, and muttering "gross" and "disgusting" at our finds, Alex and I reached the end of our mile. We left two full bags beneath one of our official Running Horse Farm "Adopt-a-Highway" sign and crossed over to the other side of the road. My shoulders ached from carrying the heavy bags, and my back was not happy with the constant bending.

Alternating carrying the last bag and picking up items as we trudged through the ditch, we finally met Amie and her friend dragging several full bags as well. Everyone was tired and cranky. We placed the last trash haul beneath the second official Running Horse Farm "Adopt-a-Highway" sign, and I drove everyone to the town gas station. As I dug crumpled dollar bills from my pocket to pay for snacks and drinks, I smiled at my crew. I think even they were proud of their efforts despite the grumbling.

The second time we combed through itchy weeds and long grass for bottles, cans, and food wrappers was easier. Hannah made us an even four in participants (Amie's friend had had enough the first time), and we paired off into partners. One carried the orange bags while the other picked up trash. Everyone wore neon yellow t-shirts I had imprinted with our Running Horse Farm and Rebel Rooster Logo instead of the ugly vests.

Cleaning our adopted ditches became another country tradition. We did it four times a year and always came away with a story or two. Like the time next to a decomposed raccoon skeleton, Hannah and Amie discovered two winning lottery tickets. (It netted them four dollars.) Another time Hannah and I worked alone and found a check for several hundred dollars; we took it to the bank who contacted the recipient who was extremely grateful we had found it. We gathered hundreds of pounds of trash throughout the years, and our local Illinois Department of Transportation folks picked up the bags for disposal after we finished our clean-ups. Because of that program, my family and friends made a difference in our little rural corner over the years, even though I still felt like a warden for my own little prison gang.

Chapter 50

I WAS PICKING RASPBERRIES one September morning when I realized something incredibly obvious. My brood was growing up. I watched from the garden as Amie and Hannah slid their lithe bodies gracefully into Alex's ancient car, backpacks carelessly slung over their shoulders. They waved goodbye to me from open windows as music pounded from his subwoofers. He revved the engine, spewing gravel with his bald tires. The lumbering yellow school bus did not stop at our house anymore.

Alex's driving skills had improved after many hours on our new mower. I had purchased it in the spring, after the John Deere sputtered, coughed, and completely died. I gave it to a neighbor who used it for parts; a shiny new orange machine took its place. It was wonderful to turn the key and not jump out of the seat because the engine backfired. The new mower's sharp blades cut grass and weeds to a consistent height and easily handled the paths in the pasture-- which was good because the old Ford 9N tractor had found a home with a different neighbor who was a mechanic. Alex and I often argued over whose turn it was to cut the grass until he got his driver's license. Then the task was all mine.

The whirlwind of my life had picked up speed again. As the kids grew older, their after-school activities increased. The pharmacy business grew in volume. Finding time to escape on the horses or my bicycle became challenging. Most of my spare moments were filled with caring for animals, preserving fruits and vegetables from the garden, farm maintenance, and trying to maintain peace between three adolescents.

"You stole my sweatshirt, Hannah. I want it back NOW!" screamed Amie from their shared bedroom the next day. I choked on my coffee as the peaceful morning shattered. Hannah sulkily tossed the hoodie in question up the stairs and stalked off to the front porch. After they left for school, I headed upstairs to take a shower only to discover Alex had used up the hot water; I shivered under a lukewarm drizzle.

The little stitched roosters gathered dust in the attic, along with train sets and stuffed animals. Amie pored over teen books and worried about boys and clothes. Alex worked on cars with his buddies. Our farm was not cool; their friends had better electronics, nicer moms, and no chores. They walked separately from me when out in public.

I relied heavily on the wisdom of Terry and Julie as I floundered in that treacherous sea of hormones. Each day brought a new crisis in the era of surliness. Sometimes after they left for school, I huddled on the couch between Harry, Sadie, Jack, and Sarah and leafed through our photo albums to reminisce of happier times before I threw all three of my offspring into the well pit. Bewildered at the speed of their transformations, I had no choice but to adapt as watching horror movie parties replaced building blanket forts and zooming down the barn hill on plastic saucers.

One positive outcome of our changing lives was their increasing independence. Alex shuttled the girls wherever they needed to go if I slid him some gas money. Babysitters were no longer required when I went horseback riding or bicycling, just notes on my whereabouts and approximate return time. I wrote and painted without being bombarded by requests for juice boxes and candy; they were all busy listening to music, reading in their rooms, or chugging milk from the carton.

I expanded my amount of canning in the fall. After two cases of pasta sauce lined the basement shelves, my counters were still full of tomatoes and peppers. The kids loved snacking on salsa with chips, so I decided it was time to make my own version. My friends discussed their recipes while volunteering Friday nights at the football concession stand; everybody had excess tomatoes that year. I dove into experimenting on my days off. Water steamed, batches cooked, and more than a few mixtures were unceremoniously dumped in the pasture because they smelled and tasted horrible.

Finally, I stumbled upon a combination that received overwhelming approval from everyone who put a chip-full in their mouth. Rebel Rooster salsa was born. Something very positive arose out of that big kettle of teenage drama we all simmered in. The formula was a closely guarded secret; only Jack and Sadie knew the process because they constantly hovered around my legs in the kitchen. I gave jars to teachers, bus drivers, neighbors and friends. Everyone loved it. Cases of it lined the shelves along with jams, tomatoes, and spaghetti sauce.

As I chopped onions and skinned tomatoes for a final batch of spaghetti sauce one fall afternoon, one of my friends carried a bucket of grapes into my kitchen. When I looked at her questioningly through the haze of onion-induced tears, she told me to follow the recipe on the pectin package for jam. Then she fled before I could coerce her into helping. I threw my vegetables in a pot, turned the burner on low, and carried her pail to the front porch.

Previously the only way I'd consumed grapes was in the fermented and bottled form. I did know they needed sorting. The good ones went into a bowl; the rotten ones that were crawling with picnic bugs went into a bucket. I spent a pleasant hour completing my task, pausing occasionally to admire the windswept green waves in the cornfields across the road. When I was done, I called our chickens over and dumped the bucket contents on the ground. Feather and Pearl immediately jumped up from their dust baths in the flower garden and raced toward me; Rusty followed. He eyed my calves as the hens pecked through the discards in the grass, waiting for an opportunity.

Moving my spaghetti sauce to a back burner, I dumped all the grapes into a kettle and added some water. The heady scent wafted throughout the entire house. Once the grapes cooked down to a pulpy mass, I strained them to remove the seeds and skins, added pectin and sugar, and cooked away. Steam condensed on the kitchen windows. Carefully I ladled the cooked jam into jars, placed seals on top and processed them in the water bath. The jam was amazing. The last grapes went into a pie (a recipe from another neighbor). Alex, Amie, and Hannah hovered in the kitchen like a pack of hungry coyotes when I pulled the pastry filled with cooked concords from the oven. I wolfed the last slice while holding the children off with a wooden spoon.

I was thankful for the bounty that the earth provided and for my country friends who shared their crops and drool-worthy recipes with me. I felt positive that we would weather the adolescent era (not always gracefully but hopefully without extensive therapy). Someday I would miss the fights and mood swings, just like I missed the sharp-edged construction toys from younger years. I wondered what my life was going to look like once the kids all flew the nest. It was approaching as fast as one of our summer thunderstorms.

Chapter 51

MY LITTLE FARM NEEDED A TOUCH of romance, something reminiscent of simple times. A tire swing had been on my wish list for years, and the stately silver maple just east of the front porch offered a perfect location to view the beautiful farmland surrounding me.

I finished my cup of coffee on the front porch and shooed Harry away from my leg. He was happily licking off the shortening I had just applied to my dry skin; it was a recommendation from a friend but an extremely bad idea around four dogs. I probably tasted like fried chicken. Walking into the house, I put on a pair of old yoga pants and wandered back outside to look for a suitable tire. There were plenty to choose from in the machine shed. Harry followed me as I rolled several possibilities out into the sunlight for closer examination. One started to roll down the lane, and I laughed as I chased it down, hoping no one was watching. It was the winning candidate.

The next step was to find a rope able to withstand our harsh weather conditions, long enough to loop up around the branch I had chosen, and strong enough to support three teenagers. After thirty minutes of searching buildings, I found a decent length of woven nylon in the barn. I shook off the dust and carried it down to the tree where the tire awaited. As I stood in the shade with the rope in my hand, I realized the job was not going to be easy. The limb I had chosen was at least fifteen feet above my head, and the ground was too uneven to support my wobbly step ladder.

The closest alternative to a bucket truck I owned was the van, so I drove it directly underneath the branch and tossed the rope while standing on the roof. It did not work well; the rope simply slithered straight back down on top of my head every time. The van's roof was slippery and did not feel very safe. I acquiesced, climbing down after the second time I slid close to the edge, and started tossing from the ground. Even after tying a big knot in one end, the rope was too wobbly and difficult to control. I needed something to weigh the end down, but not so much that it would prevent me from reaching my goal.

After moving the van out of the way, I dug through miscellaneous junk in the barn. An old dog toy shaped as a small tire had just the right weight. After looping the rope through it, I swirled the toy around like a lasso and knocked over an empty paint can and some stray boards. Under the tree, I aimed, twirled, and gave my fabrication a mighty heave. The little rubber toy flew up over my head, hit the branch, and plummeted directly toward my face. I ducked just in time.

I stepped farther away from the branch and threw again. Closer. On the sixth throw, the rope arched nicely over the branch exactly where I wanted it. But the other end was too high for me to reach, so I wiggled the rope to see if that would help. Nothing budged. I drove the van beneath the branch once more. When I stood on tip toe and reached as high as I could, my fingers were just able to close around the end. I yanked it down and let out a victory whoop.

Rolling my tire over to the dangling rope ends, I looped them through and around, tying them together in knots at the end. It felt sturdy enough when I put some weight on it, so I gingerly stepped into it and slowly swung in a circle. I put all the tools away and poured myself a celebratory glass of wine.

Stepping out onto the front porch, I smiled up at a robin-egg-blue sky. Hopping onto the tire while holding my glass, I pushed off with one bare foot and admired my farm. For each tense problem-filled moment where the world threatened to crumble around me, there was a balancing one of beauty or comedy if I looked hard enough. Thistles, thorns from hedge apple trees, and manure-caked canines could not overshadow beautiful sunrises, sweet red raspberries, and clean sheets on the line. Even my free-spirit-career-self was spending more time hanging out on the farm, whispering that wandering the world wasn't really all it was cracked up to be.

I felt an overwhelming sense of gratitude to live in such a wonderful place with three amazing children, chickens, horses and dogs. Sure, maybe Prince Charming never did materialize, but I was doing a pretty good job of learning how to rescue myself with help from the wonderful family and friends who surrounded me. Glass slippers wouldn't hold up very well in the mud and muck anyway. My life was perfect. The merlot wasn't bad either.

About the Author

PEGGY BADGETT is a mom, artist, author, birder, hiker, mountain biker, snowboarder, paddle boarder, pharmacist, and animal-loving adventurer. While raising her three children on a small Illinois farm, she penned "Pharmgirl Adventures", a local paper's Sunday column for three years. Those stories inspired her to write two books, "Romancing the Bike" and "The Rooster in the Drive Thru". After her three children flew the coop, she quit her job, sold the farm, and bought a little mountain home in the foothills of Colorado's Collegiate Peaks. She began blogging life stories on pharmgirl.org and started her business, pharmgirlstudios, which features mountain/farm scenes painted on squares of plywood and custom watercolor portraits.